Of Grace and Bombs

A Peacemaker's Iraq War Journal

by Shane Claiborne

ENGLEWOODPRESS.COM

Copyright © 2025, 2003 by Shane Claiborne

Published by Englewood Press
57 N. Rural Street
Indianapolis, IN 46201

www.englewoodpress.com

All rights reserved.

No portion of this book may be reproduced in any form without written permission from the publisher or author, except as permitted by U.S. copyright law.

ISBN 978-1-934406-26-7 (print)
ISBN 978-1-934406-27-4 (digital)

Library of Congress Control Number: 2025945203

Unless otherwise noted, Bible quotations contained herein are from the *New Revised Standard Version Updated Edition,* Copyright © 2021, by the Division of Christian Education of the National Council of Churches of Christ in the United States of America.

Cover design: Eliza Whyman

Contents

Preface	3
Original Introduction	13
Timeline	15
1. Leaving	17
2. Arrival	37
3. Presence	55
4. Return	71
Epilogue: Rutba Revisited	85
Afterword	89
About The Simple Way	93
About the Author	95

Dedicated to my mom,

who cried a lot in March 2003.

And to the mothers who are still crying.

Preface

September 11, 2001 feels like a long time ago. Many of you reading this were not alive. Some of you may not remember the Iraq War or the "shock and awe" campaign of George W. Bush, when the U.S. dropped over 900 bombs a day on Iraq while I was there. Nevertheless, this little journal is still for you. No matter how old you are or whether you have little faith or no faith, this book is for you.

This war journal is not just about Iraq or 9/11. We are republishing this new edition because we must learn from our past if we want to build a better future. As the old saying goes, "History doesn't repeat itself, but it rhymes." Today we are watching bombs fall on Gaza. It is the mass destruction of an entire group of people, and it rhymes. An attack on September 11th, 2001 paved the way to the vengeful wars in Iraq and Afghanistan, which took tens of thousands of lives. And it was an attack by Hamas on October 7, 2023, that provided the opportunity for the mass slaughter of families and total destruction of Gaza. Certainly, Israel is at the helm of this war, but the funds and weapons are being provided by the United States. It could not happen without us.

Dr. King called America "the greatest purveyor of violence in the world today." It's not a conviction that appears on many monuments or memorials and certainly doesn't get quoted by many presidents or politicians. It's worth reading the longer quote here:

> As I have walked among the desperate, rejected, and angry young men, I have told them that Molotov cocktails and rifles would not solve their problems.... But they asked, and rightly so, "What about Vietnam?" They asked if our own nation wasn't using massive doses of violence to solve its problems, to bring about the changes it wanted. Their questions hit home, and I knew that I could never again raise my voice against the violence of the oppressed in the ghettos without having first spoken clearly to the greatest purveyor of violence in the world today: my own government.

Before we write off Dr. King as being a little harsh or hyperbolic, consider this: The United States has more guns than people. We comprise about 5% of the global population but possess almost half of the world's guns. The U.S. has five times more gun dealers than McDonald's restaurants. We produce more guns than any country in the world: 9.5 million guns per year, 26,000 guns per day, one gun every three seconds. And some people still try to make the case that more guns will solve our gun problem. It's a bit like an alcoholic saying, "I've got a problem, but get me another shot of whiskey."

It's not just guns. When it comes to the death penalty, the idea is that we can try to kill people who kill to try to show that killing is wrong. The United States consistently makes the list of the most deadly countries in the world when it comes to executions. The U.S. always ranks in the top ten (and usually in the top five) executing countries in the world, a list which also includes China, Iran, Iraq, and Saudi Arabia. In 1975, the year I was born, only 15 countries had abolished the death penalty. Today, two thirds of the world—over 150 countries—have abolished it. Only a handful of countries still carry out executions, and the U.S. is one of them.

We also lead the world when it comes to weapons of mass destruction. Of the 12,000 nuclear bombs in the world, 93% are owned by two countries: the

U.S. and Russia. We have approximately half of the nuclear weapons in the world in this one country. Some of these bombs are 3,000 times stronger than "the little boy," the codename for the bomb used in Hiroshima. In fact, our nuclear bombs have the capacity of over 50,000 Hiroshima bombs. *50,000 Hiroshimas!* Not only do we possess the most weapons of mass destruction, we are also the world's biggest arms dealer. We export weapons around the world with contracts in over 150 countries. We sometimes export these weapons to countries at war with each other, literally profiting off death. Perhaps what makes us most exceptional is that we are the only country that has ever actually *used* nuclear weapons. And we did it twice in one week. There comes a point when we must recognize that this is a problem, a sickness.

We have a problem in the United States. We are addicted to violence. ADDICTED.

I've spent a lot of time in communities of folks recovering from addiction. The first step of the twelve-step program is admitting we have a problem. There are many other steps to recovery, but when it comes to healing our addictions, including our addiction to violence, we must start with acknowledging the harm we've done as a nation. We must tell the truth...and the truth will set us free. This journal is about the truth... the horrors of war we saw and documented as we lived in Baghdad. We must understand history so we don't repeat it.

Dr. King was not wrong when he called America the greatest purveyor of violence in the world. We continue to trust in our chariots and our horses, our bombs, and our guns. We continue to believe we can live by the sword without dying by the sword. We continue to choose vengeance over love as the force that will bring peace to the world, and in the face of all that, we even have the pretense to call ourselves a Christian nation. The word Christian means Christlike; more on that in a second.

I was raised in the Bible belt, down in East Tennessee. I grew up with guns, with a family of hunters and a dad who was in the military. God and country.

In high school, I helped organize "See You at the Pole" rallies, where we would gather at the flagpole before school and pray for our country. I fell in love with Jesus in East Tennessee, but the more deeply I came to love Jesus, the more I found myself at odds with much of what characterized evangelical Christianity. I still love Jesus deeply, as you will see as you read this book, and yet I am deeply troubled by how un-Christlike much of Christianity has become. Mahatma Gandhi was once asked about Christianity and he said, "I love Jesus. I just wish the Christians acted more like him." My recent work has been leading a movement called Red Letter Christians. We get our name from the Bibles that highlight the words of Jesus in red. And we like to say that we are aspiring to "live as if Jesus meant the stuff he said." Check it all out here: www.RedLetterChristians.org

As I look back on my own life, I am deeply troubled by how narrowly many Christians, including myself, have defined what it means to be "pro-life." America may be the only place in the world where you can be pro-guns, pro-war, pro-death penalty, and still say you are pro-life, as long as you get it right on abortion. It is more accurate for many pro-lifers to say they are "pro-birth" or "anti-abortion." After all, gun violence is the #1 cause of death of children in America. We can't be pro-life and ignore gun violence. And we can't be pro-life and stay silent about Gaza, where, on average, one child is killed every hour. If you were to attend a funeral a day for every child killed in Gaza since October 7, you'd be going to funerals for over 50 years.

Many of us have acted like life begins at conception and ends at birth. But it's not enough just to have a child born—we need to make sure that child thrives and has food and healthcare and education and all that they need. I'm convinced God cares about life outside the womb as well as life inside the womb—as I like to say, I am pro-life from "womb to tomb." My writing reflects this journey. I wrote *Executing Grace* about the death penalty. And *Beating Guns* about gun violence. And my most recent book *Reclaiming Life* is about the intersection of all these issues, offering a more robust framework of what it means to be pro-life. We cannot be pro-life and ignore the casualties of war in Hiroshima, or Iraq, or Afghanistan, or Gaza. Every child in Gaza is just as precious as a child anywhere else in the world. Every person in Gaza is made in the image of God. Check out our "God Loves Gaza" Campaign: www.GodLovesGaza.org

It is a deep commitment to life that led me to protest the Iraq War. It's also my love for Jesus and a genuine desire to follow Jesus that led me to Iraq. At the time, the Iraq War was the most protested war in history (as listed in *Guinness World Records*). Now Gaza is the most protested war in history. Hopefully the next war, wherever it is, will be the most protested war in history. We cannot be silent in the face of war.

One thing I do want to say clearly, though, for those of you who are not Christians: This book is still for you. I think and I hope you'll find much truth and encouragement here, even if you're not religious at all. For those of you who are spiritual but not religious, or those who are the "nones and dones," those who are tired of institutional religion, this book is for you, too. For those of you who are committed to other faiths, this book is also for you. I learned so much from my time with Muslim friends while in Iraq, and continue to have a passion for interfaith work. We must find common ground with people of all faiths as we work for peace. All of our faiths have been distorted in order to justify violence and hatred. No one kills with more passion than someone who believes God is on their side. I am grateful to all my Jewish friends who are speaking out against the violence in Gaza, at great cost. And I am so grateful for all my Muslim friends who have spoken out against extremism, at times risking their lives. Courage has many different forms. And courage is contagious.

Still, I wouldn't be honest if I didn't offer a little spiritual reflection as you prepare to read these very charged journal entries from over twenty years ago. After all, not only are lives at stake. The credibility of my faith as a Christian is at stake—especially as we see people twist scripture to justify violence.

When people are asked if they know a Bible verse, whether they consider themselves religious or not, one of the most popular answers is: "An eye for an eye, a tooth for a tooth," (Exodus 21:23). It was one of many laws given to God's people through Moses after they left Egypt. It's also one of the most misunderstood and misused verses of the Bible. It's certainly a framework that is used to justify war—like the war we see happening in Gaza right now and the war in Iraq and Afghanistan after the attacks on September 11. "What about 9/11—they attacked us? What about Hamas?"

The ancient idea was known as *lex taliones*, which means "law of retaliation." It is quite literally where we get our understanding of retaliation. It allowed a person to return harm—the same harm done to them. It is sometimes called "reciprocal justice," because you could *reciprocate* the harm inflicted on you to the person who did that harm. *Lexionus* existed thousands of years before the compilation of the Bible and as a guide to justice, it was a commonly accepted practice. It is still very common in the world in which we live. But here's what is clutch about *lex taliones*: It put clear limitations on the retaliation. It had to not just be proportional, but *exactly* the same. If someone broke your left arm, you could break their arm, but it also had to be the left arm. If someone gouges out your eye, you can gouge out their eye, but only one eye, and it has to be the same eye. If someone breaks your leg, you can break their leg, but it stops there. You can't burn down their house or threaten the lives of someone they loved. It was never meant to be a license for violence or revenge. It was meant to limit the escalating cycle of violence. Another way of thinking of it is, "an eye for an eye, but no more than that."

So limiting violence is a good thing, and it's clear that's what the original law of retaliation was intended to do: Stop the spiral of violence. You know how it goes. What starts as a tweet ends up an argument. An argument turns into a fist fight, fists turn into knives or bats or guns, and lives are lost. Or, when it comes to nations, one attack justifies an entire war with all sorts of collateral damage. If we followed the original law after 9/11, we could have made a case for killing 3,000 people in retaliation... but not tens of thousands. And in the case of October 7, Israel could make a case for killing 1,200 people, 38 of whom were children... but no one would ever justify killing 60,000 people, over 18,000 of whom are children. There would be no room for forced starvation or collective punishment.

What was meant to limit violence has too often been used instead as a license for violence. The hope was to prevent the never ending cycle of violence—to stop violence rather than validate or escalate it.

And then came Jesus. Jesus knew that ancient law, of course... and he challenged it. As a Christian I believe he came to "fulfill the law," (Matthew 5) so what Jesus did makes total sense. He said to his followers, "You have heard that it was said, 'An eye for an eye and a tooth for a tooth.' But I say to you: Do not resist an evildoer," (Matthew 5:38-39). Jesus transcends the law. His way is the law of love. As his followers, we should not hurt those who have hurt us, even if we have the legal right to do it.

We can do better than mirroring the evil done to us. We don't poke out anyone else's eye, even if they poke out ours. We don't repay evil with evil, but we return evil with good. As my mama taught me, "Two wrongs don't make a right."

So if we believe Jesus did not come to abolish the law but to fulfill the law, it all makes so much sense. Limiting violence was a good place to start. Ending violence is where this whole thing is headed. Jesus expands our ideas of justice with the law of love. Just because we can retaliate doesn't mean we should. Just because it's legal, doesn't mean it's right.

Returning harm for harm is not the best we can do. Deep down, we know we can do better than returning harm. We don't rape those who rape to show that rape is wrong. And yet, the ancient logic of *Lex talionis* is alive in well in the logic of our governments; it pervades our thinking as nations, especially when it comes to extreme events, like attacks and bombings and murder in war, we still cling to this dead-end logic that we can kill to show that killing is wrong or kill to punish killing. Somehow we think violence will heal the wounds of violence, but it only inflicts new wounds and adds to the hostile fires of hatred and revenge. In the end, we merely become the killers. We end up being the terrorists. In battling the beast, we become the beast.

It's very interesting that in the early church, a bishop named Cyprian said when a person kills another person, we all call it evil as we should, but why do we then sanctify it when the state does it in mass? Cyprian said it is wrong to kill, whether done by an individual or a president or a prime minister or the government.

Every life is made in the image of God, and we should never sanctify killing. As a Christian, I believe that Jesus is the full revelation of God. Jesus is God with skin on. In Jesus, we see unmistakably that God is love. Jesus loved his enemies so much he died for them.

God is nonviolent. God is healing the wounds of violence and sin. God is showing us the narrow way that leads to life. Throughout his ministry, Jesus disrupts systems of death, disarms violent hearts, casts out demons, and disturbs the powers that are hurting people. In the middle of an execution, Jesus interrupts the execution of a woman caught in adultery by saying, "let the one who is without sin cast the first stone." When his own disciples want to call down fire from heaven on the Samaritans, Jesus rebukes them. When his own disciple, Peter, resorts to violence, picking up the sword in an attempt to defend Jesus, Jesus scolds him and says, "Peter, if you live by the sword, you will die by the sword, put the sword away." And then he heals the person who Peter wounded.

The early Christians understood this incident as the final triumph over the logic of redemptive violence. Tertullian said when Jesus disarmed Peter, he disarmed every one of us. If ever there was a case for using violence to protect the innocent, if ever there was a case for standing our ground and resorting to violence, Peter had the strongest case there ever was. But Jesus shows all of us a better way, a way we can interact with evil without mirroring evil. Peter learned, and any of us who dare follow Jesus must also learn, that we cannot carry a cross in one hand and a weapon in the other. We cannot serve two masters. Jesus teaches and the whole New Testament affirms that we should not return harm done to us. As the early Christians said, for Christ we can die, but we cannot kill. I've come to believe we cannot reconcile any form of violence with Jesus, the Prince of peace. When Jesus said, "love your enemies," he meant we shouldn't kill them. The real question we face today is: Do we believe Jesus meant the stuff he said?

My trip to Iraq was simply an attempt to be faithful to Jesus. And to love. We were forced to ask ourselves, *Do we believe the cross offers an alternative to the sword, the gun, and the bomb? Are we willing to risk our lives for it?*

—September 2025

Original Introduction

Alright, it was tempting to add a long intro or epilogue, or to tweak things up here and there, add a few post-Iraq entries, or to change some of the stuff that seems a little outdated, maybe soften the parts that are a bit sassy, but I resisted. We've done our best to preserve these journals in their original, raw form.

I'm deeply thankful for the support of my community and friends who supported me without focusing on me, and especially my partner Michael Brix, as he circulated and compiled the e-mails I sent home from Iraq in March 2003. I am also thankful to the tireless work of folks at Doulos Christou Press who helped to create this booklet at little cost so we can spread the stories of horror and hope. And finally, the cover design was done by my brotha Scott Matney who laments this violence as only an AWOL soldier can.

May the stories stir us to the extreme acts of love and grace that these extreme times demand.

--shane (2003)

Editor's Note: Doulos Christou Press was the name under which the Englewood Review of Books published a pamphlet version of these journals in 2003. The original cover was designed by Scott Matney and featured the following image and note:

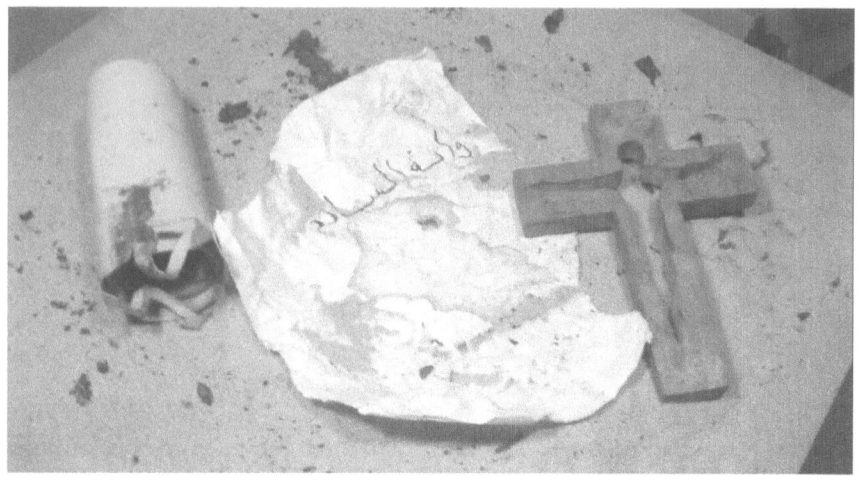

The bomb in this photo (far left) is part of a cluster bomb. This type of cluster bomb contains 202 of these deadly bomblets, each of which fractures into about 300 steel, body-piercing fragments. Each bomblet can cover an area about the size of a football field, making a cluster bomb capable of effecting a 250-400 meter region. Anywhere between 10-20 percent of the bomblets will not detonate, littering the ground until activated by animals or people. Often they are detonated by children who mistake them for toys or food, as was the case with Nasrullah, a beautiful eight-year-old boy in Afghanistan, where my friend Linda Panetta picked up this bomb.

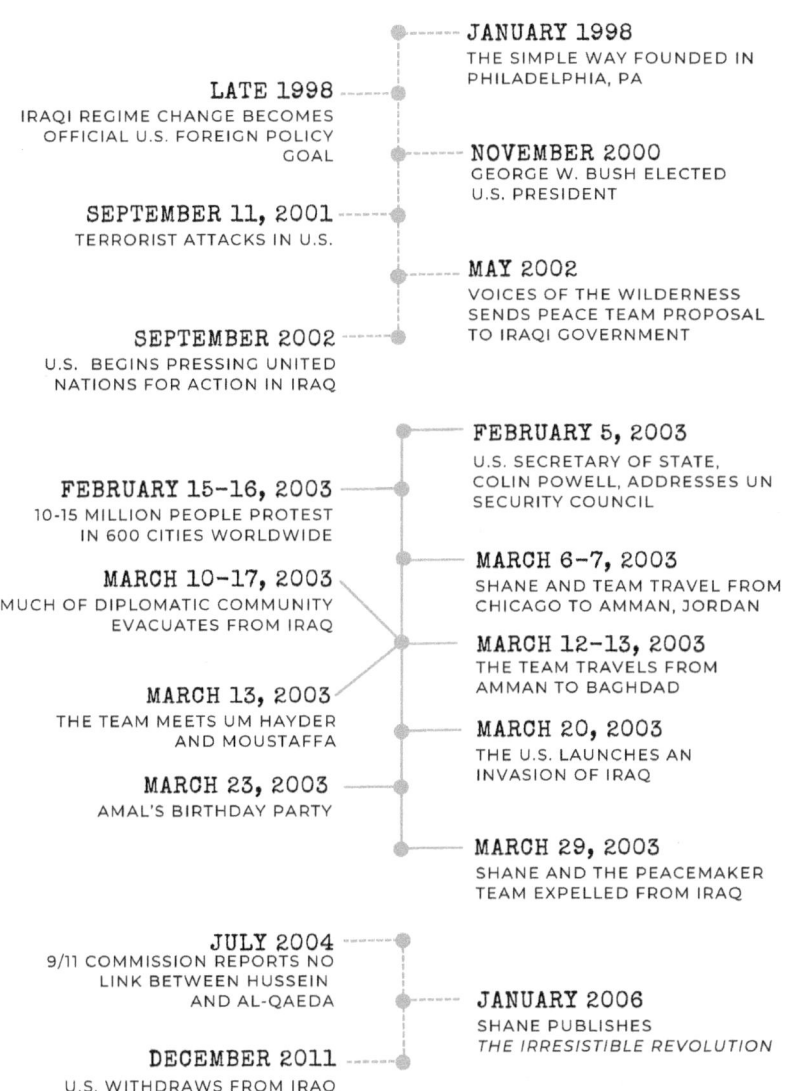

Solid line indicates events happening within the scope of the journal.

Leaving

Dear Friends,

This is mikebrix. Shane asked me to be his digital voice while he is away. Once in Iraq he will only be able to send e-mail to one address. I'll then forward the message in its entirety to you all. He wants to remind us to remain focused on families in Iraq and to mobilize to end the war. Please use his situation only inasmuch as it functions as a catalyst to bring attention to the injustice being suffered by the Iraqi people. Let's further this movement for peace. If you want to send this message on to your contacts, please do. Shane just asks that you send it in its entirety (meaning: please don't edit). If you wish to talk further about this, please call our house and talk to Brooke or Michelle. If you e-mail me back for information, I will try to get back to you, or I will forward it on to Brooke or Michelle to write you back. Please visit the websites of Voices in the Wilderness and Iraq Peace Team for more information. And, as always, you can check out Indy Media for the latest in "real" news. Alright, enough of me.

From Shane

Over the past year, I have sought God's direction regarding the crisis of our world. I felt God guiding me to Iraq, and six months ago I began blocking off March 2003 to make that possible. As the past few weeks have unfolded,

I have spent hours in prayer and fasting, surrounded by my elders who have aided in my discernment. I have considered the cost of going to Iraq, and I have considered the cost of not going to Iraq. Now, I have decided to join the incredible witness of Voices in the Wilderness, Christian Peacemaker Teams, Peaceful Tomorrows, and so many others...as I go with a delegation of a dozen people on an Iraq Peace Team. Clergy, priests, veterans, doctors, journalists, students, and concerned citizens have united with other devoted leaders such as Kathy Kelly (Nobel Peace Prize nominee), Ramsey Clark (former U.S. Attorney General), Bishop Thomas Gumbleton...to keep an ongoing presence in Iraq for over the past decade. Family members of victims killed on September 11 have gone to Iraq and are crying out to our government, "Our grief is not a cry for war...please do not kill in our name."

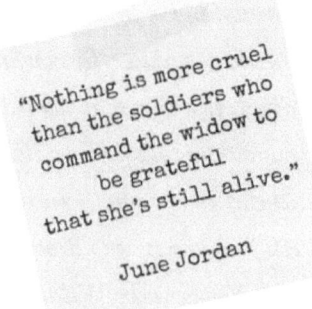

"Nothing is more cruel than the soldiers who command the widow to be grateful that she's still alive."

June Jordan

It is an honor to join these and hundreds of other voices in Baghdad with a peaceful presence of solidarity with the families of Iraq. I am thankful for my mother who stands behind me, knowing that the mothers of Iraq have children just as precious as her little one. I am also grateful to my community, the Simple Way, for supporting me without focusing on me. If you wish to remain connected to this journey, please contact my community so we can send you email updates. Now I wish to lay out a few of my reasons for going to Iraq. Feel free to circulate this as you wish, and please forward future emails to anyone you want. ~shaner

"TO IRAQ" by Shane Claiborne

I am going to Iraq because I believe in a God of scandalous grace. If I believed terrorists were beyond redemption, I would need to rip out half of my New Testament scriptures, for they were written by a converted terrorist. I have pledged allegiance to a King who loved evildoers so much that he died for them (and of course the people of Iraq are no more evil or more holy than the people of the U.S.), teaching us that there is something worth dying for but nothing worth killing for. While the terrorists were nailing him to the cross, my Jesus pleaded that they be shown mercy for they knew not what they were doing. We are all wretched, and we are all beautiful. No one is beyond redemption, and no one is beyond repute. May we see in the hands of the oppressors our own hands, and in the faces of the oppressed, our own faces. We are made of the same dust, and we cry the same salty tears.

I am going to Iraq in the footsteps of an executed and risen God. I follow a Jesus who rode into Jerusalem on the back of a donkey at Passover, knowing full well what he was walking into. This Jesus of the margins suffered an imperial execution by an oppressive regime of wealthy and pious elites. And now he dares me and woos me, come and follow, take my cross, lose my life to find it…with a promise that life is more powerful than death, and that it is more courageous to love our enemies than to kill them.

I am going to Iraq to stop terrorism. There are Muslim extremists and Christian extremists who kill in the name of their gods. Their leaders are millionaires who live in comfort while their citizens die neglected in the streets. I believe in another kingdom that belongs to the poor and to the peacemakers. I believe in a safe world, and I know this world will never be safe as long as the masses live in poverty so that a handful of people can live as they wish. Nor will the world be safe as long as we try to use violence to drive out violence. Violence only begets the very thing it seeks to destroy. My King warned his followers, "If we pick up the sword, we will die by the sword." How true this has proved to be throughout history. We armed Saddam in the conflict against Iran, and we armed Bin Laden in the struggle against the Soviet Union. Timothy McVeigh, the most terrifying domestic terrorist in U.S. history, was trained in the Gulf War, where he said he turned into "an animal."

I am going to Iraq to stand in the way of war. Thousands of soldiers have gone to Iraq, willing to kill people they do not know because of a political allegiance. I go willing to die for people I do not know because of a spiritual allegiance. The soldiers have incredible courage, courage enough to die for something they believe in. I pray that Christians would have that same courage. The command of the soldiers is handed down, rank after rank, from a human commander-in-chief clinging to the myth of redemptive violence. My mandate is straight from the mouth of my heavenly King, through the lips of the Prince of Peace—to love my enemy, and yet I still falter. May we cling to the truth that every human is created in the image of God. Do we believe the children of Iraq are just as precious as the children of New York? A love for our own people is not a bad thing, but why should love stop at the border? We, the people of Rebirth, have an allegiance that runs much deeper than nationalism.

```
Hi Simples,
I am in Mexico but thinking of you and Iraq and peace.
Everyone here that I have met is hoping and praying
for peace also. I am sending love to all, and my
thoughts are especially with Shane and all of the
people around him. I wish for many miracles.

With you in heart and spirit,
Anne
```

I am going to Iraq as a missionary. In an age of omnipresent war, it is my hope that Christian Peacemaking becomes the new face of global missions. May we stand by those who face the impending wrath of Empire and whisper: "God loves you. I love you. And if my country bombs your country, I will be right here with you." Otherwise, our gospel has little integrity. As one of the saints said, "If they come for the innocent and do not pass over our bodies, then cursed be our religion." May our lives interrupt terrorism and war, in small ways, in large ways, in moments of crisis and in everyday rhythms. These are extreme times. And I go to Iraq as an extremist for Love.

A Final Story...

The other day I was on an airline flight where I settled in next to two strangers. They began talking to each other, only to discover that they had much in common, namely political affiliation. They cracked some jokes against the liberals and boasted of the military presence in Iraq. I tried to read, tried to sleep, tried to resist the temptation of starting an intense debate which would make for a long plane ride. Finally, I got out some homemade cookies and randomly offered them to my neighbors. They continued talking about how much they traveled, all the places they've been, and they turned to me. "Where's your next trip to?" one of them asked me curiously. I got a lump in my throat (because the correct answer was "Iraq"). I paused. "Well, next week I plan to go to Baghdad."

Their jaws dropped. Puzzled, one man asked, "With the military?" I giggled. (For those who don't know me, I don't exactly fit the military prototype, with my dreadlocks and all.) "No," I replied, "I will be going as a Christian Peacemaker to be with the families there and voice opposition to the war."

I was amazed that they did NOT start arguing with me. They were intrigued that I believed in something to much that I would risk my life for it. We actually had a nice talk. And I will never forget what they said as we parted. These two people whom I had just met told me, with great drama, how "glued" they would be to the TV as they worried about me, wondering if I would make it back safely.

I stood in awe, knowing that this is the great tragedy—we have no face to war. Degrees of separation allow us to destroy human beings we do not know except as "enemy," as if Iraq was filled with millions of Saddams or Osamas and no children. So, in one hour, the walls came down a little. I thought of how powerful it was for them to have to have a face in Iraq, albeit a face these two had only met for a couple of hours on a plane. But now they hesitate as they hear the drums of war. And in the moment of hesitation, truth is birthed. Granted, I would like for my two new friends to oppose the war because of the families in Iraq, but if they oppose the war because of some goofball they met for an hour on a plane, that'll work for now.

```
Mike-
Just wanted to let you know that those of us at
Genesis are thinking of/praying for Shane as he's
in Iraq. Please let him know if you get to touch base
with him any time soon.

peace
Steve
Royal Oak, MI
```

"And now, as a captive to the Spirit, I am on my way to Jerusalem, not knowing what will happen to me there, except that the Holy Spirit testifies to me in every city that imprisonment and persecutions are waiting for me. But I do not count my life of any value to myself, if only I may finish my course and the ministry that I received from the Lord Jesus, to testify to the good news of God's grace." -Acts 20:22-24

Dear friends,

This should be the last one tonight. This is something Shane wanted me to pass on. We talked to him yesterday, and someone from Voices called today. He was in good spirits. Right now, Shane is probably in Amman, Jordan, waiting for the rest of his team to arrive. The whole team is concerned about the "Shock and Awe" campaign which Bush alluded to in his speech last night. (Which was also Michelle's birthday—send her an e-card or something!) And please keep the people of Iraq in your prayers. – mikebrix.

Iraq Peace Team, Baghdad

We write you from the brink of tragedy—a flesh and blood tragedy for the people of Iraq, a moral tragedy for the people of the U.S. We write you as the U.S. has assembled one of the mightiest war machines ever to plague this fragile and bloodied planet.

This war machine is poised to attack Iraq—a comparatively defenseless nation already crippled by years of U.N. sanctions. A nation whose misfortune, it has been said, is that "our" oil is beneath its sands. The attack—its Pentagon architects proudly call it "shock and awe"—may happen any day now. It's aimed at the cradle of much of the world's civilization. Land of the Tigris and Euphrates, land of Sumer and Babylon, land of Abraham and the Garden of Eden, Iraq is also the land of 24 million human beings—most of whom would be too young to vote or enlist if they were in the U.S. We were immensely heartened by the marches in the U.S.—and all over the world—on February 15.

We are aware that many in the U.S. will hit the streets the very day "shock and awe" commences. Given its unimaginable scale, its unthinkable carnage, "shock and awe" must, however, be stopped BEFORE it happens. Our call, then, is for PREEMPTIVE nonviolent civil disobedience in every village and city and capitol in the U.S.

Please join us. We must all mobilize all of our networks. We must all use our collective resourcefulness. We must find ways to throw sand in the gears of the war machine. The precise date of the U.S. attack is unknown, but there is reason to believe it may be very soon. The time to act is now.

Dear Friends,

We have heard from Shane. He seems well and in good spirits. Thank you for all of the prayers and thoughts to all in Iraq at this time. Again, feel free to forward these e-mails to whomever you wish, but keeping them in their entirety. Thank you. (Many personal requests for conversation, visits, and "interviews" of the simple way community simply can't happen during this time. Thank you for understanding.) Love, tsw

Notes from the Road to Baghdad

In case you haven't heard, I'm on my way to Iraq. (If you didn't get the first email outlining some of my reasons for going, please contact The Simple Way.) Our Iraq Peace Team is made up of ten people (seven from the U.S. and three from Canada). The team includes several authors, a doctor, two educators, a veteran, 2 former CIA analysts, and me.

We are currently in Jordan awaiting clearance into Iraq where we will join dozens of others (clergy, veterans, journalists, nurses, activists, lawyers...) in the international presence of peacemakers, accompanying the families of Iraq during this terrifying time. We are NOT going as human shields, but we are joining the faithful presence that Voices in the Wilderness has maintained in Iraq throughout the past ten years as they have sent over sixty delegations of Peace Teams to accompany the Iraqi families. These updates will be a little lengthy at times. Each day is filled with so much, and I often do not know when I will have e-mail access again, so read them in doses...And I will do my best to balance the laughter and tears, to keep a fair ratio of stories and politics, and to include both theological and non-theological ponderings. (Some sections will be written with non-Christian readers in mind).

A couple of stories from the road to Baghdad...

- We had a tremendous press conference in the Chicago airport as we left. As you can imagine, we drew quite a crowd. One of the men who had been watching from the margins came up to me and pulled me aside. "You are going to Baghdad?" he said, in a Middle-Eastern accent. I nodded. He grasped my hand in his, and holding it tightly, he slipped money into my palm. With tears in his eyes, he whispered "Give this to the people of Iraq." And he disappeared into the airport crowds.

- Waiting on our plane, I met a young man named Roni who is from Baghdad. We sort of hit it off. Roni was just over twenty years old, a little younger than me. He thanked me over and over for going to be with his people, and he reminded me of how youthful the Iraqi population is. UNICEF reports that 46% of the Iraqi population is under the age of eighteen—these are the faces of the Iraqi people and the faces that would suffer from a military attack. May God be with the children, for as we care for the children, we care for Christ, but for anyone who destroys these "little ones," "it would be better for him to be thrown into the sea with a large millstone tied around his neck," (Mark 9). And may God have mercy on us if we passively allow children to die in NYC, DC, or Baghdad.

- As I boarded our plane to Jordan, I prayed the Spirit would seat me next to someone interesting. (This may sound noble, but I also didn't want to sit next to a screaming child or someone who would keep nodding off and drooling on my shoulder for ten hours.) I sat down next to a beautiful Jordanian woman (at this point questioning what the Spirit was up to—ha, just kidding). So, we started talking. She told me she had been quite sick and hadn't been able to eat for days. When I asked why, she said, "Because of the war." Because of the war! While many of us look at this war with exhaustion, some with disgust, and others with deep concern...few of us are so troubled that we can no longer eat. As we continued to talk, she gave me a crash course in Arabic and taught me to write, "NO WAR." She shared how deeply moved she was that I was going to Iraq, and how she would be telling others about our trip—and that she could not wait to hear from me when I get back. (She also invited our entire team to her home in Amman for dinner—incredible.) [For those who are still wondering what the Spirit might be up to with this lovely Jordanian woman—stop wondering. She is married.] But the thing I will never forget is her name. Near the end of the conversation, she told me her name is Fida. "It means 'SACRIFICE'," she explained, and paused. "Like Jesus on the cross, or like you are going to Iraq." Thank you Fida, my prophetess—for reminding me of our call of discipleship, to sacrifice. We walk the razor edge between self-preservation and martyrdom, neither of which should be our aspirations—we follow the Lamb.

A Lenten Reflection

It is Lent. And it is Sunday morning, so I can hear church bells ringing in the distance. There are thousands of Christians here in Amman and nearly one million Christians in Iraq. Not only do they share my humanity, but they also share my Rebirth. They are my Family. ("Who is my mother, and who are my brothers?" Matthew 12). For some reason, I hadn't expected to find people here celebrating the Lenten season in such masses. So, I decided to include a little reflection for Lent—it is a little heavy, but so is the moment in which we now live. This is based on a dream I had a few nights ago.

Sometimes it is hard to sleep—so many thoughts. A bomber flew over. I looked up and could see "U.S. Air Force" on it. I tried to think only of

Jesus—a beautiful, disturbing Lover Jesus. This night, I dreamed of Jesus. At first, I could only see his back. His large, strong back was shirtless (and not as fair-skinned as I had once thought!). He was stooped over on all fours, as if he were cradling something on the ground. I wondered what it was, so I tried to get a better glance. A little head popped out from beneath his arm, giggling hysterically. Then another squirmed out from the other side. And another. How many were there?!

> Thank you so much for sharing what Shane is doing with the rest of us... I have been forwarding his emails to my entire mailing list of Eastern alumni as well as friends around the world. They are begging for more, and are taking the emails to their Bible Studies, churches, families, and their own lists. So many are praying for the team and all the families over there, as well as for hearts and minds of leaders and Americans. Please let Shane know that I am so proud of him and have tears in my eyes and my heart in my throat as I read each account... Our prayers and love are with him and perhaps it will reach through each of us that reads and passes it on. You all take care up there and let me know if there's anything you need. I will do my best to help and have others help as well. :)
>
> I love you all,
> Heather

Stooped on all fours with his arms spread wide, Jesus frantically tried to keep them gathered beneath him. There were hundreds of little faces. (Editor's note: Jesus was gigantic, not to scale. I know it's weird. Just try to hang with me; it's a dream). So, there was this huge Jesus, sprawled out above all the children. It was quite humorous. He looked like a kid frantically trying to keep a litter of young puppies from scattering. And then there was a loud crack. Out of nowhere a whip struck Jesus on his back, ripping the skin open. He yelled in pain. Then again. And again. The children began to cry. A few young stragglers ducked safely under Jesus's chest with the others. As the whip continued to strike him, rocks began to fall from the sky like hailstones—pounding on his back and bouncing off. The children huddled beneath him, sobbing. His body convulsed in agony, but he never loosened his grip on the little ones below. As the rocks kept falling, something else started to drop from the sky. These objects looked similar to the rocks, but when they hit his back, they did not bounce off like the rocks had. They sunk into his skin...and then they exploded, tearing huge holes into his back, one after another. His bones became exposed, and his body stopped moving. Blood poured off his sides and rained down on the children. *STOP! STOP! In the name of God, stop.* I could not wake up. The holes continued to tear into his flesh until the body barely resembled anything human. At last, there was silence. Stillness. Slowly the children began to stir. They crept timidly from beneath the rubble, covered with blood...but alive. And I awoke.

This season we celebrate Lent, remembering Jesus's journey into Jerusalem. But this year, I celebrate Lent in the land of Exodus, remembering our ancestors and the prophets who walked this same ground, as I make my way to Baghdad. These next few weeks, we recall the blood shed 2,000 years ago on Golgotha. And I am haunted by the uncertainty of whether the blood of Christ will be shed again in the slaughter of the Innocents in Iraq.

On Easter, we will celebrate Resurrection's triumph over the Powers of Death ("He disarmed the rules and authorities and made a public example of them, triumphing over them in it," Colossians 2:15). But will we really see the Resurrection this Easter? Or will the Powers triumph? Will the church scatter in fear, in denial, in doubt? Will only the courageous women remain at the scene of execution, to mourn?

I hope we see life conquer death, again. I am so encouraged by all the stories I hear, people of faith and conscience all over the world resisting an attack on Iraq, a people thirsty for another way of life, a creation groaning for liberation (Romans 8:22). High school and college students around the world are walking out of their classes. Entire countries have encouraged a global strike (against U.S. companies) were the war to begin. The European press has started calling global public opinion "the other superpower," announcing that if the U.S. (5% of the world's population) declares war on Iraq, they are declaring war on the Other Superpower, global democracy.

Conservatives, liberals, revolutionaries, and moderates have begun to say in one voice: A "shock and awe" attack is not sane; it was not sane in Hiroshima, and it is not sane in Baghdad. From the Pope (who we are trying to have join us in Baghdad) to Protestant bishops and regular 'ol Christians (as if there were such a thing), our church is proclaiming with integrity that this war is not within any Christian tradition, including the Just War Theory. Thank you for your courage.

May we live in the Resurrection as we disarm the Powers of Death, interrupting war with our gospel of Love.

Another little one clinging to Jesus,
shaner

To all our friends:

We actually have talked with Shane a bunch recently. (He got a deal on an Internet phone line). So, he's in good spirits and is ready for whatever God has in store for him. It was great to talk to him and lifted our spirits as well. Thanks for coming along on this journey with us. The rest of us (when we can pull ourselves away from staring at the phone, waiting for a ring) are working really hard on completing these houses. If you are in the area and can mud, sand, or paint, come on by! We work on Wednesdays, Fridays and Saturdays. If you don't live in the area, we can still use some money for the supplies! Thanks!

- mikebrix

An update from Shaner –

Thank you all for your prayers. Last night, I was up most of the night in prayer, couldn't sleep. Somehow, I had the distinct feeling we would get our clearance into Iraq today. And I have been praying, fasting...that God would lead us where we are to be...and I will follow one step at a time, clinging to Jesus. We were told by the Iraqi government that if we said we would be "human shields" we would be given immediate clearance, but we did not. (The Iraqi government has been strategically manipulating the locations of the human shields). We are going to accompany the Iraqi families, and so now we go. May God be with us and with the families of Iraq.

[Sorry (ha) if there are errors, I wrote this quickly, for we are now on our way to Baghdad. And I just heard this story from Baghdad. Our group there, the Iraq Peace Team, has been having vigils (holding signs like, "Inspections YES! Invasion NO!") outside humanitarian sites like hospitals, electric plants (imagine the hospitals without electricity), water plants, orphanages. They have just hung banners above the sites that say, "To bomb this site is a war crime," (violating Article 54 of the Geneva Convention, but precisely what was bombed in the 1991 Gulf War). Beautiful.]

"Sorry" by Shane Claiborne

Today we were given clearance into Baghdad. And this morning we were welcomed into Iraq by two of the more incredible people I've ever met—UmHayder and her 7-year-old son, Mustafa. As we were preparing for our journey, they greeted our Iraq Peace Team and invited us into their country with great joy. UmHayder and Mustafa were on their way to the United States because Mustafa needs special medical attention. We were privileged to hear their story.

On January 25, 1999, a U.S. missile was dropped on their neighborhood. Sixty-five houses were destroyed, 67 people were injured, and four died. All four of the casualties were children; one of them was Mustafa's brother. Mustafa cuddled next to his mom as she continued. Mustafa (four years old at the time) and his brother were outside playing in the street. Pieces of the missile pierced into Mustafa's body. My stomach ached as UmHayder pointed out the holes in his body today: "There is a three-inch piece of missile here," she said pointing to his leg, and another piece here in his liver...and here...and he lost most of his hand." She held up his hand which was missing all but two of the fingers. "But the Gulf War was in 1991?" we said, puzzled. How could this have happened just a couple of years ago, nearly a decade after the Gulf War? "It was a mistake." UmHayder responded, getting tears in her eyes. "The U.S. government said they were sorry for the mistake." She paused—"But now what am I to do with 'Sorry'?"

What are we to do with "SORRY"? I have become very familiar with the Arabic word for sorry—"ASIF." Over and over, people tell me how saddened they are by the U.S. war. And I tell them I am sorry for what our government is doing. But I cannot believe how, over and over, people respond, "We know the American people are not the same as the American government." They tell me how encouraged they are that so many Americans do not want to bomb them.

Today, my Palestinian taxi driver told me he knew that the U.S. was not filled with George W. Bushes, and he told me to remind my people in the U.S. that Iraq is not filled with Saddam Husseins, but with children and families, just like in America…and then he tapped my chest, grinning. "And we are brothers, my friend."

The U.S. estimates that over 140,000 Iraqis were killed or injured in the 1991 Gulf War, and at least one of every four casualties was a civilian, mostly mothers and children. I hope that we need not say "sorry" to more Iraqi mothers like UmHayder and more beautiful children like Mustafa. Perhaps someday when I say, "I am sorry for what my government is doing," people will not understand, for they will have forgotten the terror of war, and we can rid ourselves of "SORRY." War will be lost in the archives of history. May we listen to the world, and hear humanity cry out: NO…never again war. May we listen to the words of our Lover Jesus in the face of "redemptive violence"—"NO MORE OF THIS! …Put your swords away," (Luke 22:51, John 18:11). If ever there were an age to "beat our swords into plowshares," it is today. May the kingdom come on earth, and may we who expect the kingdom enact it—NOW.

So, UmHayder and Mustafa are headed to the U.S., and we are headed to Iraq. We asked her how she planned to get to the U.S. "With the help of God," she said confidently, smiling. We will join UmHayder's husband, who was a prisoner of war, and her other children in Iraq as they wonder if more missiles will fall on their neighborhood. As we travel into Baghdad, how will we make it? "With the help of God."

UmHayder and Mustafa

Booksellers' Row

Worship service, led by Iraqi women

Shane (second from left) and other members of the Iraq Peace Team

Destroyed buildings in Baghdad

Arrival

Dear Dear Friends,

This is Michael. This is a turning point in our world and our lives.

We feel the severity of the situation in Iraq with very heavy hearts. After listening to our president last night, we feel the corner has been turned. Seeing no other option available, our community will join the Iraq Pledge of Resistance and engage in non-violent civil disobedience in order to stop this war. We feel it is necessary to stand in solidarity with all those in Iraq at this time. We are praying hard for a miracle. (As Rich Mullins said, though, "Miracles are hard to come by these days.")

Over the past few days, we talked to Shane, and the team's spirits are high. He wanted me to pass along this journal entry he wrote in his hotel.

We will try to contact you all in the event of an arrest here in Philadelphia. Thank you for calling, e-mailing, and telling us you love us. This is great to hear at a time when we hear nothing but hate from our world leaders. If you are following the news, I would encourage you to balance it out with reports from independent media sources.

Peace to you all.

Shane's News from Baghdad: Nomadic Solidarity

This is a historic moment. I have never felt so much hope...and so much uncertainty. We stand on the eve of perhaps one of the most horrifying violent acts ever committed in human history. (U.S. war plans call for the "Shock and Awe" launching of 3,000 cruise missiles for Baghdad in the first 48 hours, and Pentagon officials have said civilian casualties are inevitable, comparing it to Hiroshima). And yet I wish you could see what I see on the streets of Baghdad.

There are banners crying out against the war hanging from the buildings and bridges. There are marriages and babies being born. Two nights ago, we attended an Iraqi folk festival! Tonight, we will go to a huge soccer game (and perhaps have an Iraq Peace Team vs. journalists vs. neighbors game)!

Hundreds of people have gathered here in Baghdad as a global presence of peace. I have personally met people from all over the world—Spain, Brazil, France, Canada, Australia, Belgium, Ireland, England, all over the U.S., Korea, Japan, China, Philippines, Algeria, all over. Hundreds. And dozens more are trying to get in every day, including two of our dear friends from Eastern University. As you can imagine, the people remaining here are not just your everyday goofballs. But what's crazy is they are not simply radical protestors. There are veterans, students, grandparents, Orthodox priests, Parliamentarians, Franciscan monks, evangelical Christian missionaries, lawyers, authors, professors, doctors, revolutionaries, and moderates...together proclaiming that another world is possible. It is clear that the global groaning for peace has reached a new scale. This global community, Dr. King's beloved dream, which the European press has begun calling the Other Superpower, is literally standing in the way of a war on global democracy. The Iraqi government has had (well-founded) reservations about letting hundreds of foreigners flood their streets during a war (many of us being from the aggressor nation; imagine the U.S. letting in Iraqis if we were being attacked), but they have been courageous to let so many of us in to accompany their people during this terrifying time. Hopefully, this will set a precedent for the future as the movement's momentum builds.

> Hi,
> My name is Jennifer, and I am Carolyn's aunt. I love in San Angelo, TX, and she forwarded me emails on Shane's going to Iraq. I have been praying for his safety since early last week when I was "introduced" to him and his cause. I am interested in any information you have on him and hope he is still safe somewhere at this time. I am thankful for the sites I was directed to to see what the truer news is, other than the same old drivel from CNN or Fox... It gets old as I'm sure you're aware. I hope that you're well and am thankful for this opportunity to meet online with other fellow Christians! God bless and take care. (Even tho he doesn't know me, please send my regards to Shane. Hopefully, I'll meet him someday--I have tremendous respect for him.)
>
> Thank you,
> Jennifer

What if anytime human rights are violated in our world—as in the past by the Iraqi government and in the present by the U.S. government—there is an international presence (both in Spirit and in physicality) of solidarity with those being marginalized or attacked throughout the world. (Isn't that what the church is?)

Perhaps this is the new face of global missions within the church, in an age of omnipresent war. Our movement must become mobile, fluid, nomadic. Our movement must MOVE. And it must also have permanence in the credibility of our lives, not only in crisis but in our daily rhythms. We must not be reactionary but proactive, working peacefully against tyranny and war, inequality and marginality. Just as the body's cells confine bacteria, we must confine and smother tyranny, greed, and militarism. These are indeed diseases haunting our world. They are unnatural and foreign to what we have been created for—to love and to be loved. They can only be smothered by love...not by force. Our alternative must be more attractive, and perhaps more effective, than the counterfeit freedom and imposed peace of Pax Americana.

A few glimpses of life in Baghdad...

- We went out to a street called "Booksellers Row," where Iraqi intellectuals and scholars, desperately trying to survive, have brought their books onto the sidewalk to sell in a desperate attempt to survive amidst U.S. sanctions and impending war. It was tremendous to meet them, learn from them, mourn with them. If you enjoy reading this at all, you can imagine how discouraging it was to see this...Tolstoy, Dostoyevsky, Marcuse...prostituted on the streets of Baghdad. Most books you could buy for a dollar. I couldn't decide what to do—hating to buy someone's treasures but hating even more to see such desperate poverty...I went to buy one. As I got out my money, I was swarmed by beggars. How could I buy a book?

- The Iraqi economy has been devastated by the last twelve years of economic sanctions and U.S. military aggression. Prior to 1991, Iraq was not a "third world" country; it was a developed country. In 1991, the Iraqi dollar (a 250-dinar bill) was worth about $750. Now that same bill is worth less than ten cents. You can fill your car with gasoline for less than one U.S. dollar (for 25 gallons). But how many Iraqis can afford a car?

- I just heard the most startling statement by an Air Force general, who said: "They know we own their country. We own their air space...We dictate the way they live and talk. And that's what's great about America right now. It's a good thing, especially when there's a lot of oil out there we need."

- I got to go to the hospital today. A banner hung from the entrance: "To bomb this facility is a war crime." The nurse told us there are nine new children...the others all died. None of these children will live. Because of the U.S. sponsored sanctions, they cannot have basic medications. Five thousand children die each month here from the sanctions and have been dying for twelve years. What are they dying of? Nearly all of them are dying of cancer from exposure to depleted uranium that was dropped on them in the Gulf War. Today, the statistics became a face. We laughed, and we wept. We blew up the medical gloves and made balloon animals. We juggled and colored.

- One 13-year-old child named Yassir drew us a picture—it was a snake with huge fangs eating something that looked like an egg. When we asked what he had drawn, he said, "The snake is the United States, and the egg is our world."

- Nearly every day we are invited to worship services by Iraqi Christians, Catholic, Protestant, evangelical...they feed me so much hope. One pastor has dual citizenship (in Iraq and Egypt), and he said he could take his family and go safely into Egypt, but that would betray the gospel. He committed to his congregation to stay with them through this scary time. What must it feel like to be bombed by fellow Christians who claim to have God's blessing?

- We heard the news that now 100 U.S. cities have passed resolutions opposing a U.S.-led attack on Iraq that lacks official UN support.

As NYC passed their resolution, one council member said, "Is 30 million still a 'focus group'?"

- One of my Iraq Peace Team members has hundreds of heart-shaped letters written by kids in the U.S., which are now being delivered to children in Iraq. One of them reads, "Not all Americans are bad. Please accept my apologies for what my leaders are doing."

- I would rather not die, but when I do die, I would like my death to have integrity. And if I die here I will be in good company when we get to the Gate. Moreover, if I die, that means all the children around me have likely been killed too—the shoeshine boys in the alley, the children in the orphanage around the corner...and I figure they've got V.I.P. passes into heaven. I'll just say, "I'm with them."

- Yesterday we had a picnic at one of the water treatment facilities (which provides water access to Baghdad but is likely to be bombed in an attack). We invited the workers and other friends in the neighborhood to join us for lunch. I taught one of the kids to juggle, and he taught me to sing "We Shall Overcome"—in Arabic.

A Theological Reflection... Remembering Rizpah

The other day I went to a Christian worship service led by Iraqi women. (Yes, a Christian service led by women in Iraq!) These women led about 100 of us in singing "What a Friend We Have in Jesus" in Arabic (only about three of us spoke English). Then they preached from the scriptures about heroic women in the Bible. They led us in prayer as they prayed for peace and for their children not to die in war...again. They prayed for God to heal our world and for the church to be one Body. And they wept and wept. I remembered Rizpah.

Before coming to Baghdad, many of us studied, over and over, the hidden story of a heroic woman named Rizpah (2 Samuel 21). Now it has completely new meaning as I live amongst the women of Iraq, who have seen their loved ones killed in war and face the reality of yet another attack.

Rizpah lived in time like ours. Kings were making treaties and breaking them (verse 2). The land was stained with the blood of war. In order to try to "make amends" and heal the famine that cursed them, David makes a deal with the Gibeonites. The currency he uses are human lives, as with our present war—100,000 body bags just arrived in Baghdad. He hands human beings over to be massacred...of course, they are not his own children, but children of the poor.

He takes the sons of a concubine named Rizpah, and the children are "killed and exposed before the Lord." Not only were they killed, but they were left on the hill without proper burial, left to be devoured by wild animals. And yet, despite David's best efforts, it is interesting that God does not heal the land, yet. With the reckless love only a grieving mother has, Rizpah takes sackcloth and spreads it out on a rock beside the bodies. She sets up camp. The text says she stays from the "beginning of the harvest till the rains poured," implying she was there for the season. Day after day, week after week, she protects the bodies from the animals. And word of her encampment spreads across the land...making it all the way to King David.

When he hears of her courage, he remembers Saul and his friend Jonathan. An incredible thing happens next: He is moved to gather up the bones of all the dead. Human suffering has the power to move even kings to FEEL again. Rizpah pricks the humanity of a king who had become so dehumanized, he could exchange children like currency and kill them without remorse. Then, as Desmond Tutu says, "The oppressed are freed from being oppressed and the oppressors are freed from being oppressors." And this is when God heals the land (verse 14).

I pray that if lives are lost on this hill in Baghdad, mothers would set up camp beside the bodies of their dead, and wail so loudly that word of the travesty spreads throughout the earth.

Maybe people from around the world will hear and come out with them on the rock beside the bodies. And we will come out with them on the rock beside the bodies. And we will groan together so loudly that even the kings will hear. Perhaps the kings will be moved to be human again...and then God will heal our land.

Michael-

I know you have probably received multiple other emails like this, but I just wanted to let you and the rest of the simples know that I am praying for you all and for Shane. Thank you so much for sharing all of his emails with us on the wmail list...it has been a blessing but also a burden and a challenge. Beth and I have been praying like crazy about this whole idea of war. It's something that my heart is just wrestling with... knowing that death and destruction were never God's intention for his people, but at the same time acknowledging that is will happen. I will pray for you and the others with you who are protesting and speaking out about the injustice of war, that your voices might be heard, and that Jesus's way might prevail.

Make peace. Choose Love...
Tatiana :)

Dear friends,

This is a message from Shane that I meant to direct your attention to. Sorry for the delay.

From Shane: *PLEASE direct people to my friend Wade's website. He is on my team and will be uploading pictures that parallel the stories I am telling too, and the press can use them, just give credit. Also, I am okay with press using pieces of my writing, quotes, etc., particularly secular media (indie media). I still want to make sure if things are printed or read within our Christian circles that they accurately include both the theological and the social. If they edit, make sure we (you) see the edit. Thanks.*

Love —tsw

Of Grace and Bombs by shaner

I went to worship at St. Raphael's Cathedral today in Baghdad. We sang familiar tunes, and the priest got up to give the homily. He had just served six months in prison for his faithfulness to the gospel. What would his message be, at such a crucial moment?

He told the true story of a woman whose son and husband were killed by a police officer. In court, as the judge considered the sentence of the police officer, the woman spoke forth boldly: "He took my family away from me, and I still have a lot of love to give...So I would like for him to come to the ghetto twice a month, and spend a day with me so I can be a mother to him...so that I can embrace him, and he can know my forgiveness is real."

The priest urged the listeners to love their enemies. I have heard that a million times. I have traveled across the country preaching it. But now there was a twist: The enemy he spoke of was my country. The boundaries of God's grace were being pushed once again. Somehow it didn't seem fair to tell these beautiful people, who were about to be attacked by the same enemy that killed many of their family members and decimated their city only ten years ago. We are to love those who bomb us? The priest led us to the cross, urging us to say to the Americans, "Father, forgive them for they know not what they do." He admitted that it is not based on logic—it is a love that does not make sense—a scandalous grace. And he urged this Iraqi congregation and their international friends to love those who persecute us. I wondered if perhaps our enemies will be witnesses before our Judge. Maybe as Psalm 23 says, the Lord will prepare a table before us "in the presence of our enemies," and they will be witnesses of our love. What will they say of our love? And what would dinner look like with Saddam or George W? The service ended with the singing of "Amazing Grace." And I sat in tears, wishing I could be the judge of George W. Bush. I would sentence him to spend two days a month in the Al Monzer pediatric hospital in Baghdad.

> "Somehow we must be able to stand up before our most bitter opponents and say: 'We shall match your capacity to inflict suffering by our capacity to endure suffering...Throw us in jail and we will still love you. Bomb our homes and threaten our children, and as difficult as it is, we will still love you...drag us out on some wayside road and leave us half-dead as you beat us, and we will still love you... But be assured that we'll wear you down by our capacity to suffer, and one day we will win our freedom. We will not only win freedom for ourselves; we will so appeal to your heart and conscience that we will win you in the process, and our victory will be a double victory.'"
> – Dr. Martin Luther King, Jr.

A random thought: The Franciscan priest reminded me of Francis of Assisi, with whom I have felt quite close in recent days, finding many parallels to his interruption of the Crusades by crossing enemy lines. I thought it worthwhile to recount the story. As you read, consider our current moment.

mike and simples,

Wow. Thank you so much for sending the journal from Shane. I am not sure if I have any more tears left to cry about the state of our world. I went to Circle of Hope on Sunday and the pastor was encouraging us as Christians to hold the sorrow of the world. I have been thinking and feeling that so much this week. It takes the love of Christ within us to be able to stand the sorrow and to truly hold it as the world spins with confusion, rage, pain, and disbelief. I was so moved, encouraged, and saddened by Shane's journal. I only hope that his/their presence in Iraq stands in opposition to Saddam. I know they are not naive, but I read something last week (I don't remember where) that someone said: the antiwar and peace movement is powerful and should be going strong, but Saddam needs to know that we do not support him. I think he is using it to manipulate things in many ways. I know it is worth it to be there with the people of Iraq. I just wonder if the peacekeepers can take a stand against Saddam and his tactics at the same time. I am not sure if I am making sense.

I plan to attend the march on Thursday morning at 7:30 a.m. but don't think that I will be participating in the civil disobedience. I am praying for you guys and the actions of all protestors and peacekeepers. I am still praying for a miracle as well. I will be in touch.

grace and peace,
carrie (waco/philly friend)

It was 1219, during the fifth crusade. Both Christians and Muslims were slaughtering in the name of God. War had become a necessity and a habit. Centuries of church history, where followers of the Way renounced their allegiance to the kingdom of the world and its kings, had been perverted by the seduction of "gaining the whole world but losing our soul." And then Francis had a vision of loving our enemies. He pleaded with the commander, Cardinal Pelagius, to end the fighting. Pelagius refused. (Sound familiar?)

Instead, Pelagius broke off all diplomatic relations with the sultan of Egypt, Malik-al-Kamil. The sultan in turn decreed that anyone who brought him the head of a Christian should be rewarded with a Byzantine gold piece. However, Francis continued in steadfast faith, surmounting all dangers in order to journey to the sultan. He traveled through fierce fighting in Syria and inevitably was met by soldiers of the sultan's army who beat him savagely and put him in chains, dragging him before the sultan himself.

Francis spoke to the sultan of God's love and grace. The sultan listened intensely and was so moved, he offered Francis gifts and money. Having refused the riches offered him by the sultan (of course), Francis did accept one gift—an ivory horn used in the Muslim call to prayer, which Francis later used to summon his community to prayer. (I saw the horn in Assisi!) While the sultan refused or perhaps did not dare become a Christian, he did undergo a radical transformation. He became known for his extraordinarily humane treatment of Christian prisoners during the war. One Christian prisoner wrote of the sultan, "Such kindness to enemy prisoners has never been recorded." The transformative power of grace.

Sneak peaks into Shaner's journals from Baghdad...

- I was asked by a reporter if I am scared of being here and I replied, "I am scared of NOT being here...and I am a person of faith, believing in what I do not see." Not just Baghdad, but our entire world is a scary place to be...we have made such a mess of things. But I still believe that love is more powerful than hatred, that light can invade darkness, that grass can pierce concrete. I guess I have said that soundbite for the press many times...but now it is real.

- I feel so close to the Invisible. When I walk down the streets, everything is surreal—I wouldn't be surprised to bump into the angel Gabriel—I hope he has good news! Sometimes it feels more real than the visible. It is almost mystical. I cling to the Lover Jesus. Sometimes it is hard to sleep, and I just ask the Spirit to wrap around me and rock me to sleep, cuddling. Words fail. I pray the Invisible will be more real than the visible, even if bombs fall from the sky.

- Guess who's in charge of cleaning up and watching over Iraqi oil after the U.S. secures control of Baghdad? Halliburton—Dick Cheney's former company (which left him with a huge retirement package in the tens of millions)!

- One of our "minders" (Iraqi intelligence) has been with our group for several years. Last night he met with us in a very solemn time and told us that there is an old Iraqi proverb that translates something like this: You will discover your true friends in moments of crisis. "And now," he said (in a personal, off the record, intensely moving time), "I know that you are our friends."

- I had a chance to visit the Ameriyah shelter. In 1991, it was filled with families and children who desperately packed into it for safety. It was hit with two "smart bombs." One of them hit the water tank, flooding the basement with 400-degree water, scorching the people trapped inside. Children were blown so forcefully against the ceiling that you can still see their handprints in the wall. And you can still see the scorched remains of human bodies on the floors of the shelter. This is what war looks like. I wish George Bush could spend six hours in the Ameriyah shelter. (Another tragedy is that many people are refusing to go in the shelters because they are scared of being trapped inside, remembering Ameriyah.) Outside I could hear the voices of children singing and chanting, "NO MORE BOMBS." I went out and blew bubbles with them by the graveyard of the victims who died in the shelter and joined their chorus.

- In the taxi, one of my new friends said to me today, "Pray as if everything depended on God. Live as if everything depended on you."

- One of my Iraq Peace Team members is a 73-year-old Methodist minister from Australia. His granddaughter was asked why he came to Iraq, and she replied, "My grandpa is going to comfort the Iraqi people while the Americans bomb them."

- In some cultures, you bow to show deep respect. In Iraq, if you want to express to someone that you care intimately for them, you put your hand on your heart. Over and over when we walk down the street and into the hospitals, people greet us with their hands on their hearts. Today I was struck by how similar it looks to Americans saluting the flag with their right hand across their chest. Now every time I greet these beautiful people, I consider myself pledging allegiance to them—not to their government, not to my flag, but to my sisters and brothers.

Love—another voice in the "Wildness" (as one of the hotel staff calls Voices in the Wilderness!!!),
shaner

Scenes from the Peace Encampment

Ameriyah Shelter interior

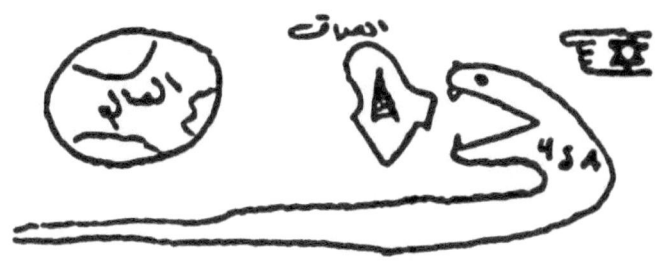

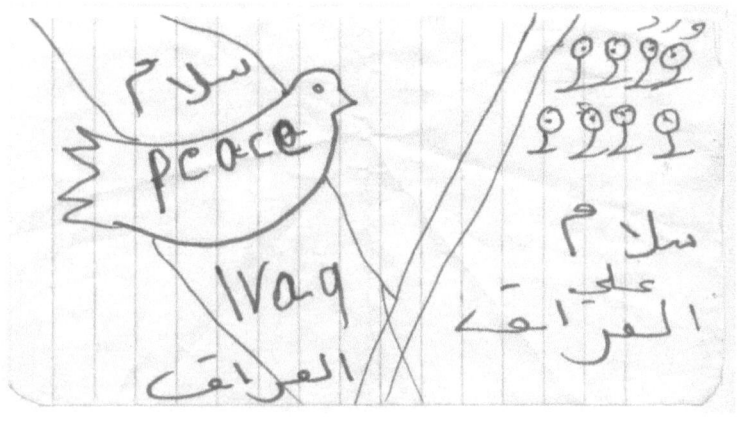

Drawings from Iraqi Children

Presence

Dear Friends –

We talked with Shane on Sunday after the School of the Americas Watch rally. The team is in good spirits, but of course they are scared. Michelle asked Shane if the "smart bombs" are really hitting only their targets. Shane's reply: "That's shit." And you know how often Shane curses.

We are really heartened by the amount of support and love that people have been pouring out on our little community. We will try to keep everyone informed as this goes on. Also, Leah and Jonathan Wilson-Hartgrove are, it's reported, in Baghdad, having arrived there sometime today.

News from Shane in Iraq

Mike – Here are the next updates. If you get them, it is only by the miracle of the Lord. Here's our best shot. Send everyone my love. It was great to talk to you. I hope to come home soon.

Here are some glimpses of life here in Baghdad. Sorry if they seem random or jumbled. We have very limited access to email and computers. So, mostly I am just able to kick out some of my journals...feel free to circulate these as you wish. And check out my friend Wade's website for pictures. I love you all desperately.

Dark Days and Shiny Shoes by Shaner

I have grown especially close to one of the "shoeshine boys," a homeless boy (about ten years old), named Mussef. The first day I met him, he was begging me for money to eat. When I stubbornly said "no" to his relentless attempts on my wallet, he turned away and muttered, "Son-of-a-bitch-mother-fucker." I whipped my head around in shock, as he took off running. Not the best first impression.

> Dear Ones,
>
> We are heavy of heart as the nation prepares for war. Please keep us in prayer as we stand in solidarity with the people of Iraq and risk arrest for non-violent civil disobedience. We love you.
>
> The simples

Day after day, we have grown on each other. We go for walks, turn somersaults, and yell at the airplanes, "SALAAM!!!" (PEACE!!!) Now every day when I walk outside, he runs at full speed, jumps into my arms, and kisses me on the cheek. And I have the shiniest shoes in Baghdad.

One day, Mussef joined our group on a walk into the center of town, carrying pictures of Iraqi children and families suffering from the war and sanctions. Press and journalists took pictures and talked to us as we stood in one of Baghdad's business intersections, and Mussef began to internalize what was happening. His shining face became bleak. Nothing I could do made him smile. As the group went home and the cameras left, we continued to sit. He motioned with his hand the falling of bombs and made the sounds of explosions as tears welled up in his eyes.

Suddenly, he turned and latched onto my neck. He began to weep; his body shook as he gasped for each breath of air. I began to cry. Somehow, I was glad all the cameras were gone. We wept as friends, as brothers, not as a peacemaker and victim. Afterwards, I took him to eat, banquet style (tipping everyone extravagantly so my guest would be welcome). Every five minutes he would ask me, "Are you okay?" I would nod, and ask, "Are you okay?" and he would nod. [Editor's note: To be honest, I think we were both scared out of our minds, but we each wanted to assure the other did not start weeping again.]

God's Encampment by Shane Claiborne

Our God dwells in tents. Certainly, it is hard to imagine in a world of million-dollar cathedrals and massive church building projects. But "God does not live in shrines built by human hands," (Acts 17). In 2 Samuel 7, we catch a glimpse of Yahweh's love for camping. King David is living in a fancy "house of cedar" and starting to think that maybe God needs a fancier dwelling place.

But God says to David, "Are you the one to build me a house to live in? I have not lived in a house since the day I brought up the people of Israel from Egypt to this day, but I have been moving about in a tent and a tabernacle." Perhaps it should have come as no surprise how deeply I have felt God among us in our tent outside the children's hospital. God camped out with the Israelites in their Exodus journey out of slavery.

God was with Rizpah as she set up camp on the rock next to her children's massacred bodies, collateral damage of kings and their wars (2 Samuel 21). Our Jesus, the baby refugee, is the one who pitched his tent among us ragamuffins and wandered the earth "with no place to lay his head." The God of tents and nomads.

Our Iraq Peace Team erected a Peace Encampment this week. We located the campsite next to a children's hospital and a water treatment plant, both of which have great significance to us. We visit the children in the Al Monzer Pediatric Hospital each day. The Al Wathba water plant provides water to the people of Baghdad and is located in a residential neighborhood (where many of the workers live). Beside our tents, we placed a banner that reads: "To bomb this site is a war crime (Geneva Convention, Article 54)." We hung up about six four-foot posters of children suffering from the war and sanctions. Each night about ten of us sleep there, and we spend time with the workers and neighbors. They have brought us blankets, fresh cookies, let us use their phone...and they stay up all night with us telling stories. When the bombs begin to drop each night, we light a candle and sing songs. Each day we go on little walks, expecting surprises.

Next to the Peace Encampment is the Lebanese Embassy, where several Embassy families live. One day they invited us, only to find out we were having tea with the ambassador! He was very interested in what is being done in the U.S. to voice opposition to the war. I told him that most of my friends were in jail in the U.S. as they interrupted the war and quoted, "In an age of injustice, the place for a just person is in jail." We laughed. I am so proud of the outcry happening around the world. Everybody back at home in Philly is in jail. One hundred seven people were arrested. Over 500 were arrested in San Francisco and 1,000 in Chicago. Our beautiful 3-year-old, Alexa, held a sign at the demonstrations reading, "Toddlers for Peace." You all are so beautiful and feed us hope.

The Mayor of Baghdad visited our Peace Encampment. With great joy, he said, "Thank you for being one with the Iraqi people."

One of the Iraqi reporters came to interview us at the Peace Encampment. Upon noticing he had a gun on his belt, we asked what kind of "reporter" he was! He said, "I am for the daily newspaper here in Baghdad, but during these times we have to be prepared for anything." I said, "Well, I hope we answer all your questions correctly." And we all got a good giggle.

Immediately after the first fleet of aircraft flew overhead, I saw a flock of geese in V-formation, reminding me that Creation is at war. After the first bombs were dropped, I could hear the desperate howling of dogs in the alley behind us. As I write this, I can hear the thunder of bombs dropping, shaking the earth. I can smell the smoke in the air, partly from the bombed ruins, and partly from the oil fires set by the Iraqi army to cloud the vision of invading aircrafts. What was a beautiful city has turned into a dull grey. The sun has disappeared. But the singing of the birds and the barking of the dogs is constant, relentless...in fact, with every thud from a bomb they only grow louder.

I can hear the bombs falling as I write this. I find myself curling up like a little child at night in a lightning storm. Every time I see a flash of light, I begin to count... "One thousand one, one thousand two..." to see how far away it is. Now when I count, I rarely get past the first, "One thous..." Hold us, Jesus. Hold the children of Iraq.

One evening at the Peace Encampment near the hospital, I was struggling to stay awake during my "night watch" shift. Then, one of the neighbors walked up to me. He was about my age, and lived around the corner with his family and children. He began to explain to me that his name was Adal, which means "Justice." He told me that justice is when things are balanced and whole. "Like when there is exactly one kilo of sugar for the one kilo weight, the scale is even."

He went on to tell me that men and women, black people and white people, made humanity balanced. Everyone is needed, Muslim and Christian, he said. Then he told me there is also a face of justice (Adal) between this world and the afterlife. God judges us accordingly. A child had just given me a flower. "Like flowers," he said. "If we make flowers on earth, we will receive flowers in the life to come."

And he pointed to the smoke in the distance from one of the bombs. "And if we make fire on earth, we will receive fire in the life to come." Then he smiled, insisting that we need to give Bush many flowers...for Bush only knows fire, and we must not let him burn up the world or himself. Later,

I read the verses of Matthew 18: "I tell you the truth, whatever you bind on earth will be bound in heaven, and whatever you loose on earth will be loosed in heaven." May we all sow flowers and smiles, for who wants to spend eternity with fire?

Today on the news we heard that one major denomination called on all soldiers to leave this war in civil disobedience and for Christians to provide sanctuary for them. Yes! I think of the communities I know of that are providing a safe place for soldiers to leave the military, providing hospitality and legal help. And I am so thankful for the soldiers who have been Reborn and who lay down their weapons in allegiance to the Prince of Peace.

Dear Friends,

The latest round of bombings in Baghdad have knocked out many communication options. We have tried to get in touch with Shane for many hours over the past few days. Tonight, before I went to bed, I checked my e-mail and (happily) there was a message from Shane. He said that he was paying someone to call our house for hours with no luck. The bombings in the city are reaching their worst yet. He went with a team to see the effects of a U.S. bombing gone awry as bombs fell into a crowded marketplace. The full story is graphic and online. Shane also said that Leah and Jonathan made it to Baghdad alright. It was a very hard ride for them as they drove past battle zones and military targets. For those of us arrested here in Philly, we are meeting on Monday at the Friends Center to discuss legal plans and the next wave of civil disobedience. Almost every day, there are marches and speak-outs and rallies against this war. Please be in continuous prayer for the safety of all in Iraq, Israel, Jordan, and the U.S. during these times. May God's peace prevail. – Michael

An Update from Shaner in Baghdad, Iraq

Most of us here in Baghdad are spending our days visiting hospitals and bomb sites (homes and neighborhoods hit by missiles), and trying to tell these stories to the press, to the church, and to the world. Here are a few stories along the way...

We have constant calls from reporters. Much of the media is sensational and melodramatic, very discouraging. So, I have decided to spend most of my time with people—in the hospitals, neighborhoods, and streets—and to rely on people I trust to spread the story of this war...like you!

> Greetings from Pittsburgh!
> I just wanted to say "Hey!" to Shane from his first employer at Eastern. I haven't kept up, except via your printed newsletters, so I didn't realize you were in Baghdad until last Tuesday night when I linked to the Electronic Iraq site from Ben Granby's MidEast Log. Anyways, I just wanted to let you know Beth and I have been praying for you, and I put the word out to our seminary listserv to all current students and alum here in Ambridge, PA as well....It's a pretty conservative crowd here (to say nothing of the rustbelt town we live in!), but I received several positive responses.
>
> I thank God that you got out safe and will continue to pray for the team members who remain, as well as for Mussef, Amal, and the others whose stories you shared. I'm sure you have much more to share than you had an opportunity to write about from Baghdad, and I look forward to hearing it.
>
> May God bless and direct you as you seek his leading for what to do next.
>
> In Him,
> Dana

I did have a live interview on CBS this morning where they asked what I thought about America, and within the first minutes they hung up on me. Hmm. They have been very interested in the dramatic fact that we could face up to twelve years in prison if we are convicted of treason...so they have been asking if we are "traitors." I wrote this little ditty in response.

Traitor?

If this bloody, counterfeit liberation is American...I am proud to be Un-American.
If depleted uranium is American...I am proud to be Un-American.
If U.S. sanctions are American...I am proud to be Un-American.
If the imposed "peace" of Pax Americana is American...I am proud to be Un-American.

BUT

If grace, humility, and nonviolence are American...I am proud to be American.
If global democracy is American, I am proud to be American.
If sharing to create a safe, sustainable world is American...I am proud to be American.
If loving our enemies is American...I am proud to be American.

REGARDLESS

I would die for the people of New York but I will not kill for them... my kingdom is not of this world.
I would die for the people of Baghdad but I will not kill for them... my kingdom is not of this world.
I will stand in the way of terror and war...my kingdom is not of this world.
I will pledge an allegiance deeper than nationalism, to my God and to my Family...
my kingdom is not of this world.
I will use my life to shout, "Another world is possible" ... for my kingdom is from another Place.

"My kingdom does not belong to this world. If my kingdom belonged to this world, my followers would be fighting…But as it is, my kingdom is not from here." – Jesus, John 18:36

Happy Birthday Amal!

We had a birthday party! One of the children we are close to, Amal, decided to celebrate her thirteenth birthday with us! So, we had a feast, grilling out in the park nearby. We played all kinds of crazy games, blew bubbles, juggled, turned flips, and ran in circles until we couldn't stand up anymore. As we were playing a little game of balloon volleyball, bombs began to explode in the background. The adults all looked uneasily at each other, but we kept playing. Then one explosion hit very close. A couple of us huddled down with the little children. I looked at this young teenager who had courage I could only dream of. She looked deep into my timid eyes and said, "It's okay, don't be scared." And she smacked me on the head with the balloon. These children were raised hearing bombs, in 1998, in 1991…and yet they will still play in a park with the people whose country is destroying theirs. Amal joked about how she might think differently about the war if Bush would bomb her school. When we asked her what she wanted for her birthday, she said, "Peace." And it wasn't because we told her to; she believed that someday people might not kill each other. As bombs continued to thunder in the background, I was reminded once again that life is more powerful than death, that children can teach old tyrants and cynics how to love. I wish George Bush could've been at this birthday party.

The Blood of Christ

God lives so clearly in the children inside the hospital…dying of the depleted uranium of U.S. dropped bombs, bodies split open by my country's war of liberation...destroying the temples. These children are God's temples. God camps out inside of our bodies. "We are...God's building," (1 Corinthians 3:9). "Do you not know that you are God's temple and that God's Spirit dwells in you? If anyone destroys God's temple, God will destroy that person. For God's temple is holy, and you are that temple," (verses 16-17). God have mercy on us.

I had a chance to visit one of the first targets of the war. She was four years old. That's exactly how the doctor introduced me to Doha, a little girl who was hit in the back by fragments of a missile and is now paralyzed. "This is the first target of the U.S. war," the doctor said with tears in his eyes. He explained that within the first ten minutes of the first bombing, Doha and her family of seven all arrived at the hospital because a U.S. missile hit their home.

We have been visiting four hospitals daily. Last week, the hospitals began to clear room for civilians injured by the war. Many of the regular patients were sent home, and many of them will die. One doctor explained, "Because of the past twelve years of sanctions, we have no medicine for pain or for cancer." As he said this, he showed us a small closet about ten feet by ten feet that held all the medical supplies for the entire hospital, with 300 patients. He continued, "Many of the patients would rather die at home with their families, and many of them are scared this hospital will be bombed again," (as it was in 1991). Within days, many of the beds have been filled by families hit by bombs.

One doctor told us that their hospital alone had brought in 108 people in three hours, and he had not slept in two days. Hundreds of people are being injured and killed, and it has only been three days. The hospitals are filled with entire families whose homes have been hit by "strategic smart bombs." I hope the world can see their faces. One seventeen-year-old boy with a big smile was hit while playing in the street with his brother. One little eight-year-old was trying to run out of the house and the wall fell on her. A one-year-old baby just died yesterday. A 64-year-old man was shopping for his family and missile fragments flew into his chest. He kept groaning, "God save us from this aggression, God save us, God save us."

friends,
Thank you for the updates on Shane. I'm sorry for the reply; I know you all are quite busy, but I had a thought to share: My church has been there through every war this country has known. When it was new, it was used by the British as a hospital during the Revolutionary War. I like to think that if the walls could talk, they would decry this war and all others; they have seen enough.

yesterday, those walls that have stood for so many years heard Shane lifted in prayer by name, and it seemed appropriate that such a strong building should echo the name of such a strong spirit.

prayers, prayers, prayers and love to you all.
erin

A mother cried as she sat next to her daughter, whose body was completely scarred and swollen from the bombs. Her daughter cried out, "Why are they killing us? What have we done?" The mother sobbed harder as she whispered that she could not tell her daughter that her sister had died from the bomb. One father held up the x-ray of his son's body, which we could see was filled with pieces of metal. And holding his son's hand, he told us, "I want the world to see my son…I want America to see his face. Maybe then they will stop this madness. What crime has he done? We did not attack the U.S., why do they attack our children?" I will never forget the desperation of another father who looked into my eyes and pleaded, "Is this liberation? Is this democracy? We are brothers and sisters to the American people. Ask them why they are killing our children. Tell them this is invasion, not democracy. Tell them if this is liberation, we do not want it."

Suppose there is a family with a very abusive father. Would it make sense to liberate the children by setting the house on fire? I believe in global disarmament. Here's a proposal: Every country should begin disarming proportionately, with each nation getting rid of a certain percentage of their weapons. The U.S. has, by far, the largest stockpile of weapons of mass destruction, with our 369 billion-dollar military budget—so we should lead the way. In fact, it would take the next 25 countries combined to add up to the military budget of the US—so let's get it started. Maybe Russia, with the second biggest military budget, would get rid of thirty billion if we'd get rid of 135 billion (50%). I am just brainstorming here; it's time to throw out some options. Let's lead the world in disarming weapons of mass destruction by turning some swords into plowshares at home. Hmmmm.

"Liberate us from this war of liberation." -One of the doctors in the Al Kindi hospital

I wish everyone could see the face of the manager of the children's hospital as he showed us the hundreds of death certificates he signed each month, for children who should not be dead.

"Violence is for those who have stopped using their imagination." -Vice President of the Al Kindi hospital, March 24, 2003.

As we continue to accompany the families here in Baghdad, I draw courage from Ruth as she stood by Naomi during tragically difficult times.

> "Do not press me to leave you, to turn back from following you! Where you go, I will go; where you lodge, I will lodge; your people shall be my people and your God my God." -Ruth 1:16

Mussef, the "shoeshine boy"

Amal's Birthday Party

Public buildings with damange from bombings;
top: elementary school (L), Iraqi home;
bottom: public market

Return

Dear Friends~

We had been sitting next to the phone for three days now, waiting to hear word from anyone who might know what was going on with Shane and his delegation, even though we had found out this morning that the phone/communication towers had been bombed a few days ago. We also knew that several peace team members were being ordered to leave Iraq, but we didn't know who those folks were or where they were from. Our emotions were on a roller coaster all day today when we heard news that Shane was leaving Iraq, then we heard differently, then no one knew for sure. This evening, though, when Michelle answered the phone, she heard Shane's tired voice announcing that he and nine others from the Iraq Peace and Christian Peacemakers Teams (including Leah and Jonathan—for those of you who know them) had made it safely to Amman, Jordan after making a "really scary" trip out of Baghdad.

We aren't sure when Shane will be arriving back in Philly. We know he is planning on going to Chicago first (where the Voices in the Wilderness office is) and then will be coming home. (Whew!) We also know that he plans to meet up with his parents at some point. It's going to be a "recovery week," so if folks could give us some time before bombarding our house with calls, we would really appreciate it. We will make sure that Shane sees all of the letters we have received from all of you, and chances are he will want to send you out a personal, "Hey, I'm back" when he returns. Thanks so much to all of you who were praying and encouraging all of us while Shane was away.

All this being said, please remember that despite Shane's safe return, there are still thousands of people, innocents, soldiers, who remain very much in harm's way as this war continues to escalate. It seems as though things are only going to get worse. Please don't allow yourself to ignore what's going on just because Shane has come home. There are still peace team members in Baghdad who are writing news/journals from the front lines and in the midst of bombs that you can keep up with, as well as keeping an eye on the independent media that is available. Don't allow yourself to become uninformed, as tempting as that may be. We know how overwhelming and exhausting it all is, but becoming numb doesn't mean the bombing, the killing, has stopped. It must stop. Thank you again for all your care. We will keep you posted...

Much much love ~ the simples

P.S. The best part of Michelle's day was being able to call Shane's mom. She will sleep tonight, after celebrating all evening...

Hello all,

We've talked with Shane a few times since he arrived in Jordan. He sent out this e-mail from an Internet café there. Also, you can find more stories about this and many other things online. Speaking of the phone...our phone bill is looking to be HUGE as we've tried to remain in contact with Shane through all of his time overseas. If you can, please consider helping us out with that. That would be much appreciated. We expect Shane to come into Philly tonight around 7 p.m. However, with international travel, and given the circumstances, that could change. We are inviting people to go to the airport with us to greet him (and Leah and Jonathan – I think they are coming in as well) and welcome them back. Give us a call for more information. Thanks!

Road of Angels...The Desert Journey to Amman

March 29—a long day for the twelve-person convoy heading for Jordan through the Western Iraqi desert from Baghdad. The morning began at about 8 a.m. loading their three vehicles, one a GMC truck and the other bright yellow taxis. The final touches of precaution were made: applying tape crosses to the cars and gathering white towels to wave out the windows. With hugs, waves, and tears, they headed off—nine members of the Iraq Peace Team (two with Voices in the Wilderness and seven members of the Christian Peacemaker Teams) along with two Japanese journalists and a Korean peace activist. Nine of them were ordered out of Iraq by the government, and two chose to leave in order to be conduits of the stories and lives they have encountered in Baghdad.

As the group headed west in the early morning light, there was ample evidence of the effects of the U.S. and British bombing: downed bridges, destroyed military and civilian vehicles strewn along the road. A few hours into the trip, they began looking for gas. One station was bombed, another abandoned. In desperation, they stopped at a final vacant station, tanks on empty, and were immediately joined by a van filled with some Somalian students leaving the University of Baghdad. Then another car joined them. Imaginations began to collaborate, and the battery of the van was used to run the gas pump, so the tanks were all filled. And they set off with renewed vigor. The roads became increasingly treacherous. Bombed out buses, an incinerated ambulance. They swerved out of the way of light posts, car parts, and shrapnel.

Soon they could see the gigantic smoke clouds from bomb hits, only seconds old in the near horizon. One of them hit only about a kilometer away. The drivers became increasingly tense, speeding up to about eighty mph to minimize the likelihood of their becoming "collateral damage" from this war. The last of the vehicles, which had fallen significantly behind the others, suddenly had a tire burst, spinning the car out of control. The car plunged into a ten-foot ditch, creating an immediate impact and flipping it onto its side.

They were able to open the doors on the top side of the vehicle and pull everyone out. Everyone was bruised, badly shaken, but conscious, though it was clear that Weldon was badly injured, and Cliff was bleeding profusely from a large gash in his head. Shane's left arm was hurt. San Hyun's face was swollen, and the driver's head and leg were injured. The first thing they noticed was a car of Iraqi civilians that had stopped to help them. (It was the first car to pass, within one minute of the accident.) Without a second thought, they piled the five additional passengers into their car and drove, heading off to the nearest town. Miraculously, a town called Rutba was only minutes away, a city of about 20,000 people located about 150 km east of the Jordanian border. As they drove to the hospital, the Iraqis pointed to a fighter jet in the sky heading toward them, and he desperately grabbed a white sheet and began waving it in the wind. The jet approached and began to turn away, leaving a trail of smoke behind it. Arriving in the town, the group was astounded to see that this civilian town, with no apparent military structures, had been devastated by U.S./British bombing. Before they could get out of the car, doctors greeted them and brought them into a small clinic with four beds. The doctors (one of whom spoke fluent English!) began immediately taking care of them, apologizing for the severe limitations and scarce medical supplies due to the sanctions. And he explained that in the past week, their town had been riddled with bombings—the communications center, the Customs building...and then with tears in his eyes he said, "Three days ago, they bombed the children's hospital." One of the men pointed to the bombed ruins only a hundred meters away. When they learned that several of us were from the U.S., the head doctor asked, "WHY this? WHY? Why is your government bombing us? Why?" In the same breath, he added with a dignified smile, "You are our brothers. We take care of everyone—Christian, Muslim, Iraqi, American...it doesn't matter. We are all human beings, sisters and brothers."

The townspeople began to gather to inspect their foreign guests, growing from a few curious neighbors to nearly thirty people. The Iraq Peace Team (IPT) group hastily offered a copy of the IPT handout, written in English and Arabic, describing their mission in Iraq. One person came in and gave them blankets. Another offered them water and smiled reservedly, motioning that it might make them sick, but was all he had. Two of the mobile IPT members began working on returning to the car to gather essentials (i.e. passports). When they inquired about going back out, the Iraqis looked at them like they were crazy. One of the doctors said, "We want to take you, but they will kill us. They will bomb our car. They have bombed even our ambulances. It is not safe for you to leave." At this point they began considering what life might be like in Rutba!

The other vehicles eventually became concerned about their missing car and pulled off to wait. After quite some time, the van of Somalians reached them. They had seen the crashed taxi and tried to see what had happened. They told the IPT members that the taxi had been in an accident, and there was much blood around, but no passengers left in the car.

Remembering the nearby town, the other cars headed back and were warmly greeted. When they asked where the hospital was, the Rutba civilian said, "The hospital is there, but it was bombed," and pointed to the clinic. Quick introductions were made, and an urgent decision to pile everyone into the remaining vehicles. Agreeing to stay in Rutba and be picked up on the way home, the injured driver gave us hugs. Then he and the doctor leaned into the window of the GMC where Weldon lay and kissed him goodbye. On the way out we tried to give the doctors some money, and they adamantly refused, insisting that they were caring for us as brothers and friends. They did have one request: "Tell the world that the U.S. bombed our hospital."

Again, they hit the road, singing and praying. But they were still not in the clear. In the distance, Leah spotted another smoke trail from a jet headed toward them. Bodies tensed and hearts cried out to God. Once again, the plane slowly steered away. They passed through more of the wreckage of war, and finally arrived at the Jordan border, after passing through the Iraqi checkpoint. They were warmly greeted by a humanitarian organization and their Somalian angels. As the Iraqi driver left to pick up the other driver and blaze the dangerous trail again, they tried to give them a tip...but the driver refused the money!

Weldon was in much pain, and they were very concerned that he might have internal bleeding, so they quickly accepted the offer of free transportation, going through the refugee camp, sharing some food, and taking a bus to Amman. At one point Weldon lost consciousness, and some Jordanian medical students came to his assistance. Others called for an ambulance, where he would be accompanied by Jonathan. Little did they know, the adventure was hardly over. The first ambulance broke down, and they were transferred to another. This one had a flat tire (it was a rough road!). After three ambulances, 14 hours after the accident, Jonathan and Weldon arrived at the hospital in Amman, where Weldon went into the ICU. He was diagnosed with broken ribs, a broken clavicle, broken thumb, and a minor head injury. The others went through the refugee camp and traveled to Amman by bus. Cliff had a final cleaning of his injury, a few more stitches, and some antibiotics. Shane's shoulder was seen to have no major fractures but some ligament damage from dislocation and was put in a sling. When they inquired about the cost of it all, one doctor offered to help with the bill. Another cut the bill nearly in half. And yet another escorted them back to the hotel, where he would later return to clean Cliff's wound.

This story is a testimony of the tremendous courage and generosity of the Iraqi people. It exemplified our time in Baghdad, in all its beauty and in all its horror. At one point we said that we were glad to be alive, and one of the doctors said, "I too am glad you are alive...but many people are dead." So, while we rejoice in God's protections and in our friends' continued recovery...we also mourn because many Iraqi families and children have not lived through this terror.

Iraq Peace Team members on this journey: Weldon Nisly, Peggy Gish, Betty Scholten, Kara Speltz, Cliff Kindy, Jonathan Wilson-Hartgrove, Leah Wilson-Hartgrove, Michael Birmingham, Shane Claiborne.

Pictures may be available from Takashi Morizumi and Shirai, the Japanese journalists who were with us. (We are working on contact info.) Korean Peace activist, Sang Hyun Bae, was part of the adventure.

Dear Friends—

I can't say thank you enough for all of the words, prayers, and calls (and money for the phone bill) that we've received over the past few months. We are extremely blessed to have you all for co-workers and friends in this amazing journey. This will probably be the last of the e-mails from us. Below are a few last thoughts from Shane, mostly in response to many requests for "home again" feelings and reflections. To everyone who came to our special return service, it was an amazing time that we truly felt. Community and Spirit—thanks for being a part of it. We love you all. ~mikebrix

From Shane:

I'm home. And I have been desperately wanting to send you all one last email and a big hug. For now, this email will have to do. Many of you have asked for my response to the war now that I am back, so I put together one last reflection here (feel free to circulate or print). It's been a very high-paced two weeks back here in Philly—lots of media work and speaking, tons of reunions, trying to sift through the lies and mourn the horror. I went home to visit my biological family (my beautiful momma!), had a press conference in Nashville and Knoxville, and a great evening presentation in Knoxville (though I got a little beat up down there in the Bible belt!). And I visited my granny and told her where I had been this month, before she saw it on the news (my new hairdo and dress clothes made it easier for her to take in!).

By the way, thanks to everyone who bought Amal's artwork! Amal is a brilliant Iraqi artist (and mother!) and a close friend of Voices in the Wilderness. I returned with a bunch of her artwork to sell, so we can send her family money, as they are now refugees in Syria. We have raised $400!!! So, thanks for those who bought her amazing work, and if you still want a piece there are a few left. Give us a call.

Mostly, I just want to thank you all. I am honored to be part of this incredible Family. Mmmm. We have letters, e-mails, gifts everywhere. Thank you for your solidarity, not just with me and the Iraq Peace Team and Voices in the Wilderness, but thank you for your solidarity with the Iraqi people suffering from this war and the past twelve years of sanctions. It has meant so much to do this adventure together, to trust all of you to get out the truth from Baghdad. Please keep crying, keep dancing, keep shouting with everything in you. Please, please keep in touch with us here at the simple way.

Thanks to Mike Brix, all the journals are on our website, and we have printed up some. If you want one, send an email. Hardcopies, too. I love you all so much. Here is one last reflection from this adventure...

"Support Your Troops" by Shane Claiborne

On the way home from the airport after returning from Baghdad, we passed a billboard that read, "God bless America and Our Military." Coming home has been a culture shock to say the least. The billboard has haunted me. As the justification for this war progressed, the "logic" became increasingly difficult to follow. The "War on Terror" lost its steam, having such weak evidence of Saddam's link to Osama or even the possibility of his regime's connection to September 11. So, the language moved to that of "disarming the weapons of mass destruction," only to find the unlikely presence of those weapons or the embarrassing truth that most likely, Saddam got the weapons from the U.S. Now the language has become one of liberation. (Or as I say, counterfeit liberation. Our team in Baghdad has told us of the graves being dug outside the children's hospital, and of their greatest fear that Americans will have seen the celebration of a few hundred Iraqi's on TV and think that this is the spirit of the five million folks in Baghdad who are solemn, angry, and skeptical). What has become strikingly clear is that the strategy for hooking the U.S. public support into the war is the extravagant deployment of hundreds of thousands of soldiers into the region. Public opinion immediately changed when they had a direct link to the conflict. The war now had a face (and the media has done their work of hiding the true Iraqi faces). People are no longer able to think theologically or intellectually or even rationally about the war, because their children are there, and that trumps any other processing.

But the price of this tactic (centered on people, many of them marginalized youth from neighborhoods like mine who see no other way to college but by joining the military) is so high, immeasurable. Human beings have become political currency. Not only is the cost in terms of dozens of dead U.S. soldiers and thousands of slaughtered Iraqis, but there is also a price for those who survive the war, who live in the ethos of the false celebration of redemptive violence. I now say, "I am not only against the war because I love the Iraqi people. I am against the war because I love the American people." "Successful" wars do not make for a safer world. Let's look at the products of "successful" war. One of the fruits of the 1991 Gulf War is a decorated U.S. Army veteran named Timothy McVeigh.

He wrote home from the war to his family and told them he felt like he was turning from a human being into an animal accustomed to killing. And then he came home, horrified, crazy...the worst domestic terrorist we have ever seen. His essays cry out against the hypocrisy of the United States accusing Iraq of stockpiling weapons when we have stockpiled the same weapons for over forty years, scorning the inconsistency of our government's outrage at Saddam's attack on Kurdish civilians after we killed 150,000 civilians in the Hiroshima/Nagasaki bombing. He saw through the lies he had been told. In some of his writing, McVeigh wrote about understanding that there was no difference between Iraqi civilians and Oklahoma City residents. No doubt his mind had been brutally deranged by being taught the way of war...so he bombed Oklahoma City in hopes that complacent Americans who numbly watch war from their TVs could see what "collateral damage" looks like and cry out against "collateral damage" everywhere. Instead, the same government that taught him to kill, kills him to show that killing is wrong. Dear God, liberate us from the logic of redemptive violence.

The only victor in war is violence. If this liberation is successful, then violence is the hero, for it was only brought about by incredible bloodshed. (I'd be glad to show you my pictures or tell you my nightmares.) Every time our government chooses to use military force to bring about change in the world, they once again teach our children the myth of redemptive violence, that violence can be an instrument for good. This is precisely the logic we are trying to rid ourselves of, especially here in the inner city. My outcry against this war is rooted in my desperate love for the kids in my North Philly neighborhood. One of them had a girlfriend who was stabbed, and he ran down our street yelling, "I am declaring war on that terrorist." War infects us. We begin to believe that violence can bring peace, in our world, in our neighborhoods, in our homes. Martin Luther King says that he continually taught rejected, angry urban youth that violence and weapons would not solve their problems but came to realize, "I have told them that Molotov cocktails and rifles would not solve their problems. But they asked, and rightly so, 'What about Vietnam?' They asked if our own nation wasn't using massive doses of violence to bring about the changes it wanted. Their questions hit home, and I knew that I could never again raise my voice against the violence of the oppressed in the ghettos without having first spoken clearly to the greatest purveyor of violence in the world today—my own government." When I got home, the kids on my block had decorated the street with sidewalk chalk that read, "NO WAR—Forever." Therein lies our hope.

The Christians in Baghdad gave me so much hope in the church. One day, I told some of our Reborn Family that I was surprised to find so many Christians in Iraq, and they laughed saying, "We were the first Christians. This is the land of your ancestors." I felt ashamed of my ignorance as I stood on the edge of the Euphrates. In our arrogance, we act as though we birthed Christianity in America, when in reality we have perverted and domesticated it. As one bishop inquired about the American church's ambivalence to the war, I tried to explain that many Christians were not sure how they felt about the war, and some even saw it as liberation. He could not even conceive of people who followed Jesus believing that this war could bring peace. He just looked me in the eyes and said, puzzled, "Then how can they be 'Christians'?" I could only weep with him.

The words of one Iraqi mother echo through my soul: "What has happened to your Christianity in America? What has happened to your God of Love and your Prince of Peace?" In this age, many U.S. Christians have let go of the cross to take hold of the flag. In fact, if you were to burn the cross, people would stare at you, but if you were to burn the flag, people would kill you. I pray that we would once again dare to follow the Way of the Cross. As we instinctively pick up our swords like Peter, I pray we would heed Christ's warning, "all who take the sword will die by the sword," (Matthew 26:52). Even before Pilate, Jesus remarks of his kingdom and his followers, "My kingdom does not belong to this world. If my kingdom belonged to this world, my followers would be fighting to keep me from being handed over to the Jews," (John 18:36).

Lover Jesus, we will trust in the way of the cross, even as the world calls us foolish. We will teach our children that it is more courageous to love their enemies than to kill them. We will teach our kids that there is something worth dying for, but there is nothing worth killing for. We will teach them that violence cannot bring peace, hatred cannot drive out hatred, and darkness cannot pierce darkness. We will support our troops by beating swords into plowshares with them. We will support our troops by providing sanctuary for them when they are Reborn and pledge the Allegiance that runs deeper than nationalism.

May we continue to enact the Way of the Cross in our world, the way of Preemptive Peace. I truly believe we are in a new era where we are not polarized into the traditional camps of "Just War Christians" and "Pacifists" in the church, of "Activists" and "Patriotic Americans" in the larger society. We are discovering the "third way" of Jesus, a new paradigm, and many new people of conscience are bypassing the unspoken and exclusive rites of passage many of us have created within the movement. Everywhere I go, there are people who may not get arrested doing civil disobedience every month, but they are quietly mourning this war and whispering, "This way of solving problems is just not right."

War might seem to work for the powerful, just as robbing a bank might seem to work for the poor—but there is a better Way that leads to life. Nearly the whole world cried out against this war, and the incredible thing is that I believe that outcry was rooted in the understanding that Saddam Hussein is a wicked tyrant, and that there is a better way to free a household from an abusive father than by burning down the house. I believe this global groaning for peace will only grow stronger. Perhaps in the days to come, we will be able to dream the dream of the other Superpower, the Beloved Community. And in the days to come, every war will be an attack on an entire People crying out for peace. One of the hospital managers put it like this: "Violence is for those who have lost their imagination. Has America lost its imagination?"

One more side note...

There are so many alternatives to this war, and while it is important to get practical, I cannot explore these in detail here, but much of the world is dreaming together. (I will be speaking to part of the U.N. next week.) These alternatives, like the International Criminal Court (which the U.S. opposed because we would also be held accountable to the court) could provide an orderly structure to charge criminals like Osama and Saddam (and others I will not name!) without violating international law by imposing things like war and sanctions. (For instance, Timothy McVeigh bombed Oklahoma City, but we did not start an embargo to starve his family or begin bombing his neighborhood.) But for these to work, it will take great humility from the United States, the humility that comes with the recognition that we are only 5% of the world's population and that if we want to hold criminals and oppressors accountable, our international criminals and oppressors in powerful places will also be accountable to the international body. Domestically, we claim to believe in democracy and justice. Do we have the courage to believe in global democracy? It is not that nonviolence has been tried and failed, but nonviolence has never been tried with as much passion and risk and money as war. Until the peacemakers have as much courage for peace as the warmakers have for war...nothing will ever change.

You are beautiful. Keep in touch.

Eat hope, drink justice, breathe peace. ~

shaner

Epilogue: Rutba Revisited

It feels important to add this little story, which was not in the original Iraq Journal because it happened a few years later. (This story was also added to the revised edition of my first book, *The Irresistible Revolution*.)

The doctors told us to "tell the world about Rutba," and we did. We told the story hundreds of times, and the Rutba House in Durham is a living witness to how that experience moved us. After returning from Iraq, Jonathan and Leah Wilson-Hartgrove opened Rutba House, hoping to offer neighbors the same type of care and hospitality we received in Rutba after our car accident.

Meanwhile, it has always been a dream of ours to visit Rutba again. Seven years later, in 2010, we got to go back. The five of us who were in the car accident in 2003 were all able to go, and we were joined by several friends, one of whom had been a soldier in Fallujah who wanted to return to Iraq as a peacemaker, and another was Greg Barrett, who wrote *The Gospel of Rutba*.

We drove that treacherous desert road from Jordan to the Anbar Province and into the little town of Rutba. When we got there, it was like something out of a movie. The whole town had gathered to greet us like royalty. They had found the doctors who had saved our lives, and we embraced with tears flowing freely. We laughed together as they explained that when they first heard we were coming back, they thought we had forgotten something valuable like a computer or a camera! But when they heard we were coming back just because we wanted to visit and rekindle the friendship, they were deeply moved. Someone did mention that there are a few militants who might want to kill us, but it was "only a few." And they slept beside our beds with AK47s to protect us. (I often laugh about how this did not fit into my theology of nonviolence, but I was grateful for their hospitality!)

And then they insisted that we had to meet the mayor of Rutba. As we met with this kind man with a warm smile, he spoke of how stories like this, and friendships like the ones we were all forging, move the world. It is not war but love that brings peace.

Then he said that he would like to see Rutba create a more permanent partnership with a city in the United States and become "sister cities." I ambitiously made the pitch for Philly. "It's the City of Love," I said. But the mayor nixed it quick: "No, Philadelphia is too big. Rutba is small. We need a small city in the US." Then he explained to us that he had been to one city in the US and he loved it. It was a little town in North Carolina that reminded him of Rutba. That town was Durham.

It was a Pentecostal moment! I started weeping, in utter shock. And I explained to him that a community had started in Durham, inspired by Rutba's hospitality, and that the community was called Rutba House.

Gleaming, the mayor declared with all the official clout warranted by his position as mayor, "Then it is done. We will be sister cities with Durham." Then he added, "And we will start a community of peace and reconciliation in Rutba, and we will name it Durham House."

This was one of the most moving and surreal experiences I have ever had. It is also one of those stories that ends with "to be continued." Rutba and the Anbar Province continue to be one of the most troubled corners of the world, making communication next to impossible and travel there equally difficult. So keep it all in your prayers. And if you meet someone who has $100,000 lying around, we'd love for them to help rebuild the hospital that was bombed. Until then, we'll keep telling the story of Rutba, and we'll keep living out the love they showed us in that magical little town.

The story is a testimony to the tremendous courage and generosity of the Iraqi people. They have also reminded us not to tell it in a way that makes the experience seem extraordinary or exceptional. And they are right. Arab hospitality is something we experienced over and over again. I am convinced that had we wrecked in another town, there would have been another "Rutba" around the corner.

Afterword

I am convinced, especially as I read over this journal again in September 2025, that we cannot wait around for the next war or international crisis. We have to be organizing and working every day for peace. As Dr. King said: "Those who love peace must learn to organize as effectively as those who love war." The Iraq war was the most protested war in history...until Gaza. Now we see people all over the world standing up for life, insisting that more violence will not heal the wounds of violence. There is another way. We must protest. But we also have to "protestify"—we have to cast a vision for a better world.

The prophets speak of a world where we beat our swords into plows and our spears into pruning hooks, a world where we turn the tools of death into tools of life and "study war no more." It's that vision that inspired us to begin transforming guns into garden tools—on the 10th anniversary of 9/11 in 2011.

We thought to ourselves, *Well, we don't have a lot of swords in America, but we have a whole lot of guns, more guns than people.* So we invited people to surrender their weapons, to disarm, and to allow us to repurpose their guns into garden tools.

Our first donated gun was an AK-47, a gun I saw everywhere in Iraq. It is one of those weapons of war that is still legal on our streets here in the U.S. We took that AK-47 and turned it into a shovel and a rake. And we have been turning guns into garden tools and other lifegiving things ever since. Hundreds and hundreds of guns have been transformed through the national network of RAWtools (www.RAWtools.org). We get our name from flipping

"WAR" around, naturally. And as we've done this holy work, folks have sent us photos and stories from around the world. Guns turned into guitars in Mexico. Assault rifles transformed into saxophones in Mozambique. A bicycle made from guns, and a menorah made from guns after an attack on a synagogue. We even have a "Peace Mic," a microphone made from melted gun metal that really works, so folks can share their stories, poems, songs, and dreams for a better world!

Several years after my time in Iraq, I had the opportunity to go with a delegation to Kabul, Afghanistan. We were hosted by a group of young people there who had read Dr. King and Gandhi (translated into Farsi). They shared this vision of a world where we turn from war and destroy our weapons, a world where we study war no more.

Every time we transform a gun we are declaring, "All things can be made new." I sometimes show my evangelical friends a shovel made from a gun and say, "This is what a gun looks like when it gets 'born again.'" And what is true of metal is also true of human beings. A person who has killed another human being can also be transformed. No one is beyond redemption. Metal that is crafted to kill can be transformed. So can people. So can policies. I keep thinking of those words of the doctor in Iraq: "Violence is for a world that has lost its imagination." It is time to reimagine the world.

I've learned a lot about the prophets from scholars like Abraham Heschel and Walter Brueggemann. Walter, a dear friend who recently passed away, spoke often of "the prophetic imagination" (also the title of his classic book). Rabbi Heschel and Walter have helped me understand that we often get the prophets wrong. We often think of them as fortune tellers, trying to predict the future. But that's not quite it. The prophets were not fortune tellers, they were truth tellers. And they were not trying to predict the future. They were trying to change the future by waking us up in the present, and insisting, "IT DOESN'T HAVE TO BE THIS WAY." The prophets invite us to imagine the world and to begin building a different future than the one we are building right now. Another world is possible. We don't have to keep living by the sword and dying by the sword, living by the gun and dying by the gun, living by the bomb and dying by the bomb.

That iconic passage about turning guns into plows (Isaiah 2) ends by saying, "Nation will not rise up against nation... people will study war no more."

But what strikes me is that peace does not come from the top down, but from the bottom up. Just like water boils. Peace does not begin with the politicians and presidents, with the kings and prime ministers... they are the ones who keep starting the wars.

Peace begins with the people of God, who are tired of death and violence. It is the people who lead the politicians to peace. It is the people—the prophetic conscience of the State—who become so fed up with violence that they take things into their own hands. And they begin to destroy their weapons and turn the tools of death into tools of life.

May we have the courage. May the Spirit give us the prophetic imagination that these desperate times demand. *Amen.*

It feels right to end this war journal with the words of a war veteran named George Mizo. These words were shared with me at a vigil for peace. I think of them often, especially as we continue to build a movement that includes veterans and military service members who have experienced the other impact of war—the moral injury that happens to those who have held the guns, dropped the bombs, and taken other people's lives. (The organization I help lead, Red Letter Christians, has hosted forums featuring soldiers who have become conscientious objectors and refused to kill—and we have a whole section of resources on our website: https://redletterchristians.org/conscientious-objector-resources/)

You, my church, told me it was wrong to kill ... except in war.
You, my teachers, told me it was wrong to kill ... except in war.
You, my father and mother, told me it was wrong to kill ... except in war.
You, my friends, told me it was wrong to kill ... except in war.
You, my government, told me it was wrong to kill ... except in war.

But now I know, you were wrong... and now I will tell you—my church, my teachers, my father and mother, my friends, my government—it is not wrong to kill except in war. It is wrong to kill.

Shane Claiborne
September 2025

About The Simple Way

In 1995, dozens of homeless families moved into an abandoned Catholic church building in North Philadelphia. They were told by the Archdiocese that they had 48 hours to move out or face arrest. With nowhere to go, these courageous mothers and children hung a banner on the building that said, "How can we worship a homeless man on Sunday, and ignore one on Monday?" They held a press conference announcing they talked with the building's real owner (the Lord Almighty!) who said they could stay until they found somewhere else to go. That was the spark that lit the fire of The Simple Way.

A few years later, some students (including Shane and five other Eastern University graduates) who had been a part of that movement pooled their money and bought 3234 Potter Street. They made an old shoe repair store their home. Before long, they grew into other abandoned houses on the block.

Many of the early experiences of The Simple Way are found in Shane's 2006 book, *The Irresistible Revolution*. After over two decades, the intentional community has become a nonprofit organization—a little village of neighbors sharing life and working together.

Shane, his wife Katie, and son Eli live across the street from the original Simply Way house, which now serves as a hub for all the work in the neighborhood.

Adapted from www.thesimpleway.org.

 Shane Claiborne is a prominent speaker, activist, and best-selling author. Shane worked with Mother Teresa in Calcutta, and founded The Simple Way in Philadelphia. He heads up Red Letter Christians, a movement of folks who are committed to living "as if Jesus meant the things he said." Shane is a champion for grace which has led him to jail advocating for the homeless, and to places like Iraq and Afghanistan to stand against war.

Now grace fuels his passion to end the death penalty and help stop gun violence. Shane's books include *Jesus for President, Red Letter Revolution, Common Prayer, Follow Me to Freedom, Jesus, Bombs and Ice Cream, Becoming the Answer to Our Prayers, Executing Grace*, his classic *The Irresistible Revolution, Beating Guns*, and his newest book, *Rethinking Life*. He has been featured in a number of films including "Another World Is Possible" and "Ordinary Radicals." His books have been translated into more than a dozen languages. His work has appeared in Esquire, SPIN, Christianity Today, TIME, and The Wall Street Journal, and he has been on everything from Fox News and Al Jazeera to CNN and NPR. He's given academic lectures at Harvard, Princeton, Liberty, Duke, and Notre Dame. In 2023, Shane received the prestigious The King Center's Beloved Community Award for Social Justice from Dr. Bernice King (daughter of Martin Luther King Jr. and Coretta Scott King).

Shane speaks regularly at denominational gatherings, festivals, and conferences around the globe.

Thank you for reading!

If you enjoyed this book, please leave a review on Amazon or your favorite online retailer.

Also Available from Englewood Press:

The Cultviating Communities Series

Englewood Press is a partnership between The Englewood Review of Books and Cultivating Communities. Learn more at www.englewoodpress.com

www.ingramcontent.com/pod-product-compliance
Lightning Source LLC
Chambersburg PA
CBHW060536080526
44586CB00012B/762